Public Sector Reform:
What Works and Why?

An IEG Evaluation of World Bank Support

http://www.worldbank.org/ieg

2008
The World Bank
Washington, D.C.

Cover: Mural *El Buen Gobierno,* by Diego Rivera (1924). Courtesy of Universidad Autónoma de Chapingo, where this mural appears in the Administration Building.

ISBN-13: 978-0-8213-7589-1
e-ISBN-13: 978-0-8213-7590-7
DOI: 10.1596/978-0-8213-7589-1

Library of Congress Cataloging-in-Publication Data have been applied for.

World Bank InfoShop
E-mail: pic@worldbank.org
Telephone: 202-458-5454
Facsimile: 202-522-1500

Independent Evaluation Group
Knowledge Programs and Evaluation Capacity
    Development (IEGKE)
E-mail: eline@worldbank.org
Telephone: 202-458-4497
Facsimile: 202-522-3125

 Printed on Recycled Paper

Contents

Central post office in Morrocco. Photo by Julio Etchart, courtesy of the World Bank Photo Library.

Abbreviations

AAA	Analytical and advisory activities
ACT	Anticorruption and governance (transparency)
BEEPS	Business Environment and Enterprise Performance Survey
CAS	Country Assistance Strategy
CEM	Country Economic Memorandum
CFAA	Country Financial Accountability Assessment
CPAR	Country Procurement Assessment Report
CPIA	Country Policy and Institutional Assessment
CSA	Civil service and administrative (reform)
DPL	Development Policy Loan
DFID	Department for International Development (United Kingdom)
DPR	Development Policy Review
EITI	Extractive Industries Transparency Initiative
ESW	Economic and sector work
GAC	Governance and anticorruption (strategy)
HIPC	Heavily indebted poor countries
IBRD	International Bank for Reconstruction and Development
ICRG	International Country Risk Guide
IDA	International Development Association
IDF	Institutional development funds
IEG	Independent Evaluation Group
IGR	Institutional and Governance Review
IMF	International Monetary Fund
MTEF	Medium-term expenditure framework
NGO	Nongovernmental organization
OECD	Organisation for Economic Co-operation and Development
OPCS	Operations Policy and Country Services
PEFA	Public Expenditure and Financial Accountability
PER	Public Expenditure Review
PETS	Public expenditure tracking surveys
PFM	Public financial management
PIU	Project implementation unit
PPAR	Project Performance Audit Report
PREM	Poverty Reduction and Economic Management Network
PRSC	Poverty Reduction Support Credit
PSG	Public sector governance
PSM	Public sector management
PSR	Public sector reform
SAL	Structural Adjustment Loan
TAX	Tax administration (reform)
WBI	World Bank Institute
WDR	World Development Report

Government building in Hanoi, Vietnam. Photo © Galen Frysinger.

Acknowledgments

This evaluation of the World Bank's support for public sector reform was prepared by the Country Evaluation and Regional Relations division in the Independent Evaluation Group (IEG).

The team was led by Steven Webb and comprised Milka Casanegra (tax administration), Corky de Asis, Tim De Vaan, Anne Evans (civil service and administrative reform), Odd-Helge Fjeldstad (anticorruption), Ilka Funke (assistant team leader), Gita Gopal, Ina Hoxha, Keith Kranker (database and statistical analysis), Evelina Mengova (database), Victor Orozco (database and statistical analysis), Vikki Taaka (logistics and document handling), Rajiv Joseph Tharian, Gemi Thomas, Sofia Valencia, Richard Webb (history), and Clay Wescott (public financial management). The country case studies were prepared by de Vaan, Funke, Hoxha, Orozco, Tharian, Webb, and Wescott. Helen Chin, Heather Dittbrenner, and William Hurlbut assisted with editing.

The team received guidance and support from the IEG management team—Shahrokh Fardoust, Ali Khadr, and Vinod Thomas—and in the initial stages work from Ajay Chhibber, Lily Chu, and Kyle Peters. Cheryl Gray, Director of IEG World Bank during the final phases of preparing the evaluation, recused herself from management oversight because of her earlier key role in the public sector reform agenda.

Colum Garrity, Gregory Kisunko, and others on the Public Sector and Governance Sector Board were generous in helping gather information.

The peer reviewers—Catherine Gwin, Roumeen Islam, and Marcelo Selowsky—gave useful suggestions at several stages of the process, as did several other colleagues in IEG.

A panel of external advisors—Professor Shankar Acharya (Indian Council for Research on International Economic Relations), Professor Francis Fukuyama (School for Advanced International Studies, Johns Hopkins University), and Dr. Ngozi Okonjo-Iweala (until November 30, 2007, of Brookings Institution)—gave useful inputs at several stages of the evaluation. Professors Acharya and Fukuyama provided a joint comment on the report going to the Committee on Developmental Effectiveness. The generous financial support of the Norwegian Agency for Development Cooperation (Norad) is gratefully acknowledged.

Director-General, Evaluation: *Vinod Thomas*
Senior Manager, IEGCR: *Ali M. Khadr*
Task Manager, IEGCR: *Steven B. Webb*

Government building in Yaroslavl, Russia. Photo © Linda Garrison/cruises.about.com.

Foreword

World Bank support for public sector reform has grown notably in recent years. To address the questions of what is working and why in this area, the Independent Evaluation Group has examined Bank lending and other support for public sector reform in four areas: public financial management, administrative and civil service, revenue administration, and anticorruption and transparency.

A majority of countries that borrowed to support public sector reform improved their performance in some dimensions, but there were shortcomings in important aspects. Middle-income borrowers saw improvements in their public sector quality more frequently than low-income borrowers, even though the low-income group usually had greater needs for public sector improvement.

Performance usually improved for public financial management, tax administration, and transparency, but not for civil service. Direct measures to reduce corruption—such as anticorruption laws and commissions—rarely succeeded, as they often lacked the necessary support from political elites and the judicial system.

Analytic work, including the development of monitorable indicators, was especially useful in financial management, but such analysis was usually absent in the civil service and administrative area, which contributed to the differences in outcomes.

The Governance and Anticorruption Strategy approved by the Board in 2007 and being implemented now proposed actions that could address concerns raised in this evaluation. The recommendations of this evaluation highlight directions that deserve priority.

First, it pays to recognize the especially complex political and sequencing issues in public sector reform projects. That in turn puts a premium on understanding the political context, identifying the prerequisites to achieve the objectives, focusing on the basic reforms initially, and being realistic about the time it takes to get significant results.

Second, the priorities for anticorruption efforts need to be based on an assessment in each country of the types of corruption most harmful to development. Sustaining efforts to reduce corruption have better prospects when they emphasize making information public and building country systems to reduce the opportunities for corruption.

Third, it is important to strengthen the civil service and administrative components of public sector reform. This effort includes providing a better framework and indicator sets for quality of civil service. Although the difficulties of civil service reform have led to some calls for abandoning this area, the evidence indicates that improved civil service is essential for major improvements in other areas. Successes with some aspects of civil service have shown what is possible.

Vinod Thomas
Director-General, Evaluation

Segment of mural *El Buen Gobierno* by Diego Rivera (1924). Courtesy of Universidad Autónoma de Chapingo, where this mural appears in the Administration Building.

Executive Summary

The effectiveness and efficiency of a country's public sector is vital to the success of development activities, including those the World Bank supports. Sound financial management, an efficient civil service and administrative policy, efficient and fair collection of taxes, and transparent operations that are relatively free of corruption all contribute to good delivery of public services.

The Bank has devoted an increasing share—now about one-sixth—of its lending and advisory support to the reform of central governments, so it is important to understand what is working, what needs improvement, and what is missing. To address these questions, the Independent Evaluation Group (IEG) has examined lending and other kinds of Bank support for public sector reform (PSR) between 1999 and 2006 in four areas: public financial management, administrative and civil service, revenue administration, and anticorruption and transparency.

Although a majority of countries that borrowed to support PSR experienced improved performance in some dimensions, there were shortcomings in important areas and in overall coordination. The frequency of improvement was higher among International Bank for Reconstruction and Development (IBRD) borrowers than among International Development Association (IDA) borrowers. Performance usually improved for public financial management, tax administration, and transparency, but not usually for civil service. Direct measures to reduce corruption—such as anticorruption laws and commissions—rarely succeeded. Recommendations of this evaluation focus on improving guidelines for civil service and anticorruption reforms and on setting realistic objectives and sequencing of reforms.

The public sector is the largest spender and employer in virtually every developing country, and it sets the policy environment for the rest of the economy. About one-sixth of World Bank projects in recent years have supported PSR (see figure ES.1) because the quality of the public sector—accountability, effectiveness, and efficiency in service delivery, transparency, and so forth—is thought by many to contribute to development. Improving the efficiency of government counterparts is also essential for the effectiveness of the Bank's support for development.

Two themes of this evaluation correspond to the primary dimensions of the public sector: how it manages finances over the budget cycle and how it organizes and manages its employees—their recruitment, pay, and promotions. A third theme—tax administration—is a part of the public sector that the Bank has often supported with special projects or components. The fourth theme of the evaluation—anticorruption and transparency—has cross-cutting issues that appear in the other thematic areas and also in special components of some PSR projects. (Anticorruption components of sectoral projects are outside the scope of this evaluation, as are decentralization and legal and judicial reforms.) Forty-seven percent of IBRD borrowers and 74 percent of IDA borrowers in the period 1999–2006 had one or more projects with components in at least one of these four areas.

The evaluation team assembled and analyzed a database that combined information on all borrower countries and on the more than 460 projects that since 1990 have focused on PSR in one or more of the four thematic areas. The team also did in-depth studies of 19 countries, including field visits to 6, and supplemented this with information from IEG's recent country evaluations.

The knowledge of outcomes is imperfect, because of measurement problems and the long lag between the start of reforms and seeing their full effects. Nonetheless, public sector performance on some key dimensions seems to have improved in a majority of cases where there have been Bank lending and analytical and advisory activities. But outcomes vary substantially across country types and thematic areas. Success or failure of PSR in any country is determined mainly by government actions, but Bank actions have also contributed.

Patterns of Bank Support for PSR

Almost all countries received some analytical and advisory assistance (AAA) on public sector issues over 1999–2006, but coverage varied by theme. Most IDA and blend countries had extensive AAA, and three-fourths had PSR lending, including policy-based projects. For instance, Burkina Faso had nine PSR loans, including eight development policy credits, with major components in all four thematic areas, plus six AAA products.

About half of IBRD countries had no PSR lending in the period 1999–2006, and about a quarter had two or more loans. In most IBRD countries, the Bank stayed engaged, even with problem governance states. It did so through AAA or lending if the countries wanted it; the lending was usually associated with considerable improvement in the public sector performance.

The higher frequency of PSR lending to IDA countries reflects both a greater need in these countries for PSR and stronger pressure from the Bank and other donors to conduct PSR.

Among countries getting PSR lending, more than 80 percent of IBRD borrowers and 69 percent of

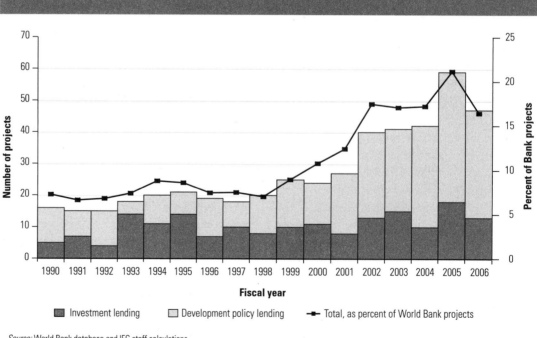

Figure ES.1: Lending Projects with Significant PSR Components, 1990–2006

Legend: Investment lending / Development policy lending / Total, as percent of World Bank projects

X-axis: Fiscal year (1990–2006)
Left Y-axis: Number of projects
Right Y-axis: Percent of Bank projects

Source: World Bank database and IEG staff calculations.

IDA borrowers showed improved performance. Country cases identify three factors contributing to success in the different areas:

- *Being realistic about what is politically and institutionally feasible,* as well as being opportunistic in preparing technical foundations for what might become feasible in the future. In Bangladesh, the Bank supported preparatory work on difficult areas of civil service and anticorruption when substantive reform was not on the table. These later proved useful when a reform-minded government came to power.
- *Recognizing that enhancing technology is not enough by itself, that the most crucial and difficult part is changing behavior and organizational culture.* In Ghana, for instance, implementation of the integrated financial management system stalled until attention turned to changing behavioral patterns and incentives.
- *Dealing with the basics first,* such as ensuring that taxpayers have unique identification numbers before installing a complex collection system or ensuring that the government is executing a one-year budget reasonably well before launching sophisticated multiyear budgeting. Some projects in Bulgaria, Cambodia, Guatemala, the Russian Federation, and Sierra Leone did this relatively well. In many countries, however, the policy-based lending conditions were across the board and exceeded the government's technical or political implementation capacity. Projects in Ghana, Guatemala, Guyana, Honduras, and Indonesia had difficulty because they went straight to sophisticated measures, such as installing accrual accounting, when the personnel capacity was not ready and the government was not successfully administering cash accounting.

Variation across Themes

Public expenditure and financial management was almost always a component in PSR loans. Public financial management—managing the money from budget planning, to procurement, treasury functions, and monitoring—has often been the leading edge of PSR, in both the diagnostic and lending phases of Bank support. In this area (and in tax administration), the ministry of finance has usually been given strong support, and the Bank's analytic tools have become the most systematic and widely accepted.

About two-thirds of all countries that borrowed for financial management showed improvement in this area in a Bank-wide data set (the Country Policy and Institutional Assessment), and it was the most consistent area of improvement in the case studies. Budget formulation and reporting usually received more attention and had more success than the downstream phases of the spending cycle, such as procurement and auditing.

Fiscal crises often initially motivated governments to seek financial management help from the Bank, and the projects examined usually succeeded in resolving the fiscal crises and making recurrence less likely. To improve the effectiveness of spending, however, the criteria and loan conditions have been harder to specify.

The Bank's diagnostic work on financial management has contributed to the effectiveness of lending in this area. Public Expenditure Reviews are now more frequently participatory or are government led and give more attention to institutions and the implementation of the budget. The Public Expenditure and Financial Accountability (PEFA) indicators have made an important advance by laying out a framework for all aspects of public budgeting and financial management, a framework agreed to by donor and borrower countries. They are monitorable and actionable— the government can observe and affect them directly.

Civil service and administrative (CSA) reform has been the second most common area of PSR lending. Although CSA performance has improved in fewer than half of the borrowing countries, improving CSA has been essential for sustaining PSR in other areas. The urgent issue of affordability of a wage bill often led to emphasis on retrenchment and salary adjustments that were politically unrealistic. This approach typically failed to improve public administration, as noted in a 1999 IEG evaluation

(IEG 1999). Since then, the Bank has advocated the same approach, with similar lack of success in some countries, such as Cambodia, Honduras, and the Republic of Yemen; elsewhere, however, it has had some success by focusing more on personnel management reforms, such as merit-based recruitment and promotion, to improve performance and counter patronage-based systems.

The frequent failures of CSA reform, despite continued acknowledgment of its importance, seem to reflect the lack of a coherent strategy (with isolated exceptions) and of clear diagnostic tools to address CSA issues. Along with the inherent political difficulty, the weak diagnostic work on civil service seems to be one reason reform projects in this area have less success than financial management reforms. AAA on civil service is less than one-fourth as common as for financial management, and it did not precede lending in most case study countries.

Bank projects for tax administration have generally succeeded and benefited from strong government ownership, particularly by ministries of finance, and from good diagnosis and strategy (often led by the International Monetary Fund). More than three-fourths of countries with investment projects for tax administration improved their performance. In the areas of tax administration, IDA countries with investment projects had higher rates of improvement than IBRD countries. For countries with a fiscal crisis, tax administration reform was an attractive entry point, particularly in former Eastern Bloc countries.

Attention to anticorruption and transparency in country strategies and lending programs has grown since the late 1990s. A majority of the borrowers for PSR have increased transparency but not reduced perceptions of corruption. Even after 1997, when direct approaches were no longer taboo for the Bank, lending usually supported indirect measures against bureaucratic corruption—reducing opportunities for corruption by simplifying procedures and regulations, moving to e-government in various areas, and rationalizing personnel management. These had some success. Direct meas-

ures to reduce corruption—such as anticorruption laws and commissions—rarely succeeded, as they often lacked the necessary support from political elites and the judicial system.

The Bank has helped develop tools to improve transparency and reduce bureaucratic corruption, such as the Public Expenditure Tracking Survey, quantitative service delivery surveys, and the Business Environment and Enterprise Performance Survey. In Bulgaria and the Indian state of Orissa, direct anticorruption measures helped make public service delivery more efficient and accessible to citizens while staying within the bounds of political feasibility. Some government-wide transparency efforts, such as access to information laws and implementing agencies and the Extractive Industries Transparency Initiative, also show promise as tools against state capture, but it is too soon to see results.

The Bank's diagnostic work on corruption and transparency generally follows a separate track from other public sector areas, focusing on global perceptions or the experience of the private business sector and giving less attention to the extent of corruption in the core public sector. Most Country Financial Accountability Assessments and Country Procurement Assessment Reports have not dealt adequately with risks of corruption in those systems. Institutional and governance reviews rarely analyzed the political factors contributing to corruption, although their saliency is widely acknowledged.

Despite its mantra of "no one size fits all," the Bank has not developed a framework that adequately recognizes the long duration of the process to reduce corruption and the differences in where countries need to start. As steps in the process, experiences in Nigeria and Cambodia suggest that reducing the development cost of corruption (including eliminating it in Bank-supported investment projects) is politically feasible and valuable for development. Still, the Bank's stance against corruption needs operational clarification in country contexts—for instance, how the extent of corruption should affect the balance between investment and budget-support operations.

Sequencing and Coordination across Themes

The evidence does not support either of two positions taken by some observers—that PSR is too difficult to be worth trying or that public sector issues are so interlinked that only comprehensive solutions will work. Many PSR projects have succeeded, although usually not immediately. To realize the full benefits of improving public service delivery and accountability, PSR must eventually lead to substantial improvement across the board, including the civil service; modest and selected entry points can have partial success and can lay the basis for later progress.

Starting with AAA has been a successful way for the Bank to develop a trusting relationship with governments to work on sensitive areas of PSR. In Egypt, a reformist government requested Bank support for anticorruption after an Investment Climate Assessment in 2006 identified corruption as a major barrier for business. Often a Public Expenditure Review with financial management emphasis was a good starting place, as in Bangladesh, Ethiopia, Tanzania, Uganda, and several Indian states.

The Bank has improved the integration of AAA and lending in the various aspects of public financial management, but not across the full range of PSR themes. Results are better where arrangements are institutionalized to coordinate staff in diverse sectors within the country program (as in the Latin America and Caribbean Region, with the sector leaders in close proximity to country directors). Otherwise, coordination occurs less regularly, when there happens to be alignment of personalities, skills, and schedules.

Recommendations

Design PSR projects and allocate Bank resources to them with recognition that PSR has especially complex political and sequencing issues. Be realistic about the time it takes to get significant results, understand the political context, identify prerequisites to achieve the objectives, and focus first on the basic reforms that a country needs in its initial situation. Reconsider the balance between development policy and investment lending; institutional change usually needs the sustained support of investment projects, although development policy lending can help secure the enabling policy changes.

In country PSR strategies, set priorities for anticorruption efforts based on assessments of which types of corruption are most harmful to poverty reduction and growth. Only when the country has both strong political will and an adequate judiciary system should primary emphasis be on support for anticorruption laws and commissions. Given that reducing corruption will be a long-term effort, the Bank should emphasize two things: building country systems that reduce the opportunities for corruption that are most costly to development and making information public in ways that stimulate popular demand for more efficient and less corrupt service delivery. The country team needs operational clarification about how the Bank's anticorruption efforts fit within the overall country strategy.

Strengthen the CSA components of PSR, giving them a better framework and indicator set, and give more attention to the budget-execution phases of financial management. This will require PEFA-like actionable indicators for CSA performance and more linkage between the implementation of reforms for civil service and for financial management.

Government building in Nairobi. Photo from picasaweb.google.com.

Management Response

Management welcomes this Independent Evaluation Group (IEG) evaluation of World Bank support for public sector reform (PSR), covering the period from 1999 through 2006. Management sees much on which it can build from the review's findings. However, it would like to make a few observations on the review, relative to recent strategy and policy changes. Last, management broadly concurs with the recommendations, with some nuances and clarifications.

Concurrence with the Broad Thrust of the Analysis and Recommendations

The evaluation contains a number of important conclusions that management welcomes in the context of its overall assistance to countries in PSR. Specifically, management appreciates the findings on the long-term nature of PSR, the conclusion that an incremental approach can produce results, and the usefulness of economic and sector work (ESW) up front. It will build on these in work going forward.

PSR requires time

Management notes IEG's finding that many PSR projects have succeeded, although often not immediately. The key lesson is to be realistic as to timing. That fact has implications regarding the lending products that best support PSR. In many cases, a programmatic approach using a series of loans, notably Development Policy Loans (DPLs), linked to a government's medium-term program has proven successful (see, for example, World Bank 2007a). As noted in the review, specific investment operations, either in parallel with DPLs or self-standing, can provide a longer time frame of support. Country context will determine the exact mix.

Incremental approach

The IEG review concludes that support through modest and selected entry points can have par-

tial success and can lay the basis for later progress, including in difficult areas such as civil service reform. That fits with management's view that PSR needs strong country ownership and that the Bank needs to tailor its assistance to the country's pace of reform. It also reinforces the point above with regard to lending instruments.

Usefulness of ESW

The IEG review notes the benefit of up-front ESW. It credits good diagnostic work in public financial management (PFM) as having contributed to successful outcomes of Bank support. In particular, it cites Public Expenditure Reviews and the Public Expenditure and Financial Accountability (PEFA) indicators as useful in this regard. Management notes the potential value of prior ESW with regard to support for countries that want to undertake civil service reform.

Management Observations

Management has just a few issues that it would like to raise with regard to the analysis in the review. These issues are related to governance and anticorruption, to analytic and advisory activities (AAA) work on PFM, and to the evolution of Bank support over time, learning the lessons of experience. Management also acknowledges that greater progress needs to be made on civil service and administrative reform but notes that the outcomes are weaker in poor governance environments and stronger in better governance environments, as measured by the Country Policy and Institutional Assessment.

Governance and anticorruption

The Bank does thematically classify a portion of its support as "other accountability/anticorruption." However, as emphasized in its new Governance and Anticorruption (GAC) strategy, management sees corruption as an outcome of poor governance (World Bank 2007c). Support for better governance—and so for reduced corruption—is being mainstreamed across the Bank's entire portfolio, including in traditional investment operations. Though this is recognized in the IEG review, from some of the discussion, a perception might be that the review is of the Bank's anticorruption agenda rather than that subset of the agenda that can usefully be addressed through PSR. For instance, the IEG review does not evaluate treatment of GAC in country assistance strategies, GAC in sectors, or GAC in projects or global partnerships on GAC. The World Bank Group's overall approach to anticorruption is best discussed in the context of the strategy cited above. Management has committed to report to the Board in 2008 on progress in implementation of this strategy.

Demand side of support for good governance and anticorruption

The report points to possible missed opportunities for supporting the demand side of good GAC. Management would point out that in many cases, countries have incorporated innovative measures into sector projects supported by Bank lending that helped develop the demand for good governance—for example, expenditure tracking surveys, beneficiary surveys, and citizen scorecards. Understandably, the purely sectoral operations with these components were beyond the scope of the IEG review.

Scope of public financial management AAA

Management would like to reiterate its different view on one point—whether Country Financial Ac-
countability Assessments (CFAAs) and Country Procurement Assessment Reviews (CPARs) should incorporate more diagnosis of corruption issues. CFAAs and CPARs typically identify aspects of country PFM systems that might facilitate corruption (such as off-budget accounts, inadequate financial management and procurement information systems, weak regulatory environments, inadequate systems of internal control and internal audit, poor capacity of implementing agency staff, excessively complex financial administration rules leading to poor enforcement, and "cash rationing"). Management considers this coverage of corruption issues appropriate. Given the complexity and multifaceted dimensions of the corruption issue, neither detailed corruption diagnostics nor the development of anticorruption strategies can be undertaken as part of the CFAA or CPAR per se. That said, as part of its overall work on implementing the new strategy, management is developing stronger linkages with corruption issues in the Bank's PFM work, recognizing that PFM systems are an important instrument in a country's anticorruption agenda and also that PFM performance is affected by the overall corruption environment.

Learning the lessons of experience

Management notes that the review covers seven years. During that period, many of the lessons cited in the IEG review have been taken into account in Bank work, notably regarding development policy operations (DPOs). The Bank extensively reviewed its experience with adjustment lending, held wide consultations, and moved in 2004 from adjustment to DPOs (World Bank 2004b). That change was more than just in name and incorporates many of the suggestions that the IEG review highlights—including the importance of strong country ownership, a long-term approach to policy reform taken in realistic incremental steps, customization, and a sharp reduction in the number of conditions to just those critical for the success of the reform (normally taken in advance of Board approval of the operation—one indicator of ownership). One of the reasons for these changes was to better position the Bank to help countries strengthen public sector institutions. Under DPOs, the type of conditions has changed, notably toward measures to strengthen public sector management, and the number has fallen significantly (World Bank 2007a).

Conclusion

Overall, management warmly welcomes this evaluation from IEG. Management generally accepts IEG's recommendations. Detailed responses to the recommendations are outlined in the Management Action Record.

Management Action Record

Recommendation	Management response
Design PSR projects and allocate Bank resources to them with recognition that PSR has especially complex political and sequencing issues. Be realistic about the time it takes to get significant results, understand the political context, identify prerequisites to achieve the objectives, and focus first on the basic reforms that a country needs in its initial situation. Reconsider the balance between development policy and investment lending, because institutional change usually needs the sustained support of investment projects, although development policy lending can help secure the enabling policy changes.	**Ongoing/Agreed.** Bank management agrees in principle with this recommendation, noting that it points to the importance of intensifying AAA upstream of PSR operations— which can have significant budget implications. How the recommendation can best be implemented will require learning by doing and will depend on country context. To implement the GAC strategy, the Bank's regional Vice Presidential units have identified 26 countries that currently are initiating country-specific country GAC strategy processes—including, in some of these countries, intensified governance assessments that aim to, among others, identify political obstacles to reform and feasible approaches to sequencing. At the conclusion of this learning process, Bank management is committed to reporting to the Board whether and how it intends to systematize and scale up its GAC work, including AAA. Reporting on the agreed actions will be done in the context of overall GAC reporting.
Within country PSR strategies, set priorities for anticorruption efforts based on assessments of which types of corruption are most harmful to poverty reduction and growth. Only when the country has both strong political will and an adequate judiciary system should the Bank put primary emphasis on support for anticorruption laws and commissions. Given that reducing corruption will be a long-term effort, the Bank should emphasize (i) building country systems that reduce the opportunities for corruption that is most costly to development and (ii) making information public in ways that stimulate popular demand for more efficient and less corrupt service delivery. Provide operational clarification to the country team about how the Bank's anticorruption efforts fit within the overall country strategy.	**Mostly agreed.** Management agrees with the recommendation that the most effective way in which PSR can support anticorruption efforts is by giving priority to work on country systems and on information flows to the public. As the recommendation suggests, the more complex challenge (which goes beyond the scope of PSR operational work) has to do with the relationship between country strategies and operations more broadly and anticorruption efforts. Management's response to this broader challenge has been laid out in the strategy, "Strengthening World Bank Group Engagement on Governance and Anticorruption" (World Bank 2007c). Three ways in which GAC strategy implementation addresses this broader challenge are (i) by signaling that GAC is not only a PSR concern but "is everybody's business"; (ii) by intensifying efforts to manage fiduciary and other GAC risks in Bank operations; and (iii) by underscoring that approaches to addressing GAC are country specific and should be derived from poverty-reduction priorities. With regard to IEG's request for operational clarification, this last point implies that attention to GAC issues generally will be most intensive in those sectors that are given priority for poverty reduction in country strategies. The GAC implementation progress report to the Board, to be presented in 2008, will report on experience.
Strengthen the CSA components of PSR, providing them with a better framework and indicator set, and give more attention to the budget execution phases of financial management. This will require PEFA-like actionable indicators for civil service and administrative performance and more linkage between the implementation of reforms for civil service and for financial management.	**Ongoing/Agreed.** Bank management agrees with the recommendation that a better framework is needed for the civil service and administrative components of PSR work. A strategic staffing exercise, being undertaken as part of GAC strategy implementation, will help implement this recommendation. The Poverty Reduction and Economic Management anchor already has begun recruiting to strengthen its staffing on civil service and administrative reform. Under the GAC strategy and implementation plan, intensified work is under way within that anchor to develop a new generation of "actionable indicators," with indicators for civil service and administrative a top priority. However, as is evident from the seven-year experience of developing the PEFA indicators—cited as a success in the IEG evaluation—the development of new and better indicators is a challenging task that will take time. For the budget execution phases of financial management, Bank management notes that both the PEFA indicators and the CFAAs give them strong attention. An earlier, narrower focus on budget formulation has already has been incorporated in the Bank's operational work. Management will monitor and report on progress on these actions in reports to Executive Directors on the implementation of the GAC initiative.

Chairperson's Summary: Committee on Development Effectiveness

On March 26, 2008, the Committee on Development Effectiveness (CODE) discussed the evaluation of World Bank support for public sector reform and the draft management response.

Background

Key strategy documents include "Strengthening World Bank Group Engagement on Governance and Anticorruption" (World Bank 2007c) and *Reforming Public Institutions and Strengthening Governance: A World Bank Strategy* (World Bank 2000). The update on implementation of the 2000 Bank strategy was prepared in April 2002, and it was also reviewed in 2005 as part of the Sector Strategy Implementation Update, which was discussed by CODE. The Independent Evaluation Group (IEG) evaluations related to public sector reform (PSR) include "Country Financial Accountability Assessments and Country Procurement Assessments Reports: How Effective are World Bank Fiduciary Diagnostics?" (IEG 2007), considered by the CODE Informal Subcommittee in 2007; and "The Impact of Public Expenditure Reviews: An Evaluation" (IEG 1998) and "Civil Service Reform: A Review of World Bank Assistance" (IEG 1999), which were considered by CODE in 1999.

Main Findings and Recommendations

IEG reviewed the Bank support for PSR between 1999 and 2006 across four themes—public financial management (PFM), civil service and administration (CSA), revenue administration, and cross-cutting anticorruption and transparency initiatives. One of the key findings was that performance in at least one dimension of PSR improved in a majority of countries that borrowed for core public sector activities. IEG also noted that outcomes of PSR lending were better in PFM and revenue administration, but less successful in CSA. It found that direct measures to reduce corruption rarely succeeded, and it was more effective to strengthen systems and increase transparency. IEG identified three factors contributing to better performance: realism about what is feasible; attention to behavior and organizational culture as well as incentives that are underlying drivers of reform; and focusing on the basic issues first. The need for a Bank framework that recognizes the long-term process required to reduce corruption and the different starting points of countries was noted. IEG's main recommendations were as follows: (i) recognize the complex political and sequencing issues in the design of PSR projects and allocation of resources; (ii) set priorities for anticorruption efforts within country PSR strategies based on an assessment of which types of corruption are most harmful to poverty reduction and growth; and (iii) strengthen the CSA components of PSR.

Draft management response

Management found that the report offered rich insights. It appreciated the manner in which the evaluation was undertaken and the dialogue with IEG on different aspects of PSR. Management was encouraged by the improved performance in a majority of countries that borrowed for PSR, although it also recognized that there was no room for complacency. Although broadly agreeing with the thrust of the analysis and recommendations, management commented on the treatment of the anticorruption agenda, support to the demand side of governance and anticorruption, and scope of the analytic and advisory activities related to PFM. It cautioned that the IEG evaluation may be perceived as a review of the Bank's anticorruption agenda rather than of PSR that contributes to reducing corruption. Regarding more diagnosis of corruption issues through the Country Financial Accountability Assessments (CFAAs) and Country Procurement Assessment Reports (CPARs), management considered that there is adequate coverage in these diagnostic assessments, which typically identify aspects that might facilitate corruption. It remarked that work was ongoing to develop stronger links with corruption issues in the Bank's PFM work. Management noted that many lessons emerging from this evaluation report have been taken into account in the Bank's PSR work.

Overall Conclusions and Next Steps

The Committee welcomed the clear and well-written evaluation and the positive response from management. Noting the central importance of PSR to the Bank's work, members were gratified by the improvements in performance in countries receiving International Bank for Reconstruction and Development or International Development Association resources for PSR. There was broad agreement with the main findings and recommendations, and members agreed on the importance of political commitment, complexity of sequencing, and the need to sustain efforts over the long term, especially to change organizational culture and behavior in support of PSR. Although the Bank has demonstrated comparative advantage in PFM, a member cautioned against excessive focus in this area. The importance of a holistic approach to address the broader and more fundamental issue of government effectiveness—including of CSA and the delivery systems for various public services/functions—was emphasized. Some members emphasized the need for selection criteria based on the Bank's comparative advantage vis-à-vis other actors. There were several comments about support for CSA and anticorruption and the advisability of a more nuanced approach than a simplistic direct effort. Other interventions related to the need to consider the sustainability of PSR improvements; the progress in the Bank's knowledge of PSR support since the World Development Report (WDR) of 1997, whose findings are echoed in the report; the link between PSR and poverty reduction; and internal institutional issues, including incentives and instruments to better support PSR. Better understanding of PSR issues based on comprehensive international experience, and the need for candor in evaluation and learning from failures, were recommended.

The following main issues were raised during the meeting.

Challenges of PSR

Given the central importance of PSR to the Bank's work and the complexity of PSR, speakers were encouraged by the Bank's performance in this area. Members generally concurred with IEG's findings and emphasized the need for a country-specific approach; government ownership and political will; time and patience for organizational culture and behavioral changes; coordination with other donors; and an opportunistic and realistic approach and appropriate sequencing for PSR. A member remarked on the paradox of PSR support, which can build capabilities but may not lead to an increase in government effectiveness; it was suggested that IEG could further explore this dichotomy in future evaluations. *Management commented that the Bank was attempting to increase government responsiveness and effectiveness in public service delivery by encouraging beneficiary participation in implementing, monitoring, and providing feedback.* Another member highlighted that PSR outcomes depend on both the Bank's and the government's efforts and emphasized that IEG needs to be clear that it is evaluating the Bank's and not the government's performance. *IEG clarified that the evaluation's primary focus is the effectiveness of the Bank's programs, but there is a strong country context that needs to be considered.* The issue of how the Bank may bring about government commitment, political will, and behavior changes was raised. A member suggested that the Bank can only increase capacity and knowledge, which can lead to change. Questions were also raised on how to ensure sustainability of efforts and what the link between PSR and poverty reduction is. *Management sought to ensure sustainability by establishing models of success that would increase interest and political commitment for further reforms. Based on limited data, IEG found that sustainability had been more likely in PFM and tax administration than in CSA and cross-cutting anticorruption initiatives. Management and IEG commented on the links between PSR and poverty reduction, which is the final outcome (for example, greater budget transparency leading to predictable flow of resources for service delivery, and better targeting of social spending).*

The challenges of addressing CSA, which must be done country by country, go beyond the introduction of merit-based systems and could benefit from a long-term "in-service" approach. A member sought clarifications about IEG's reference to the "ingrained patronage systems" and whether this is applicable to all countries. *IEG clarified that CSA initiatives often did not succeed because of difficulties in removing resistance to reforms and indicated that it would take a careful look at the language in the final report.* It was expected that country teams would have a better understanding of the context in which PSR support, including for CSA, would be implemented. In view of the complexity of PSR, a few members stressed the importance of sharing experiences and lessons learned. Some speakers were interested in learning not only from successful experiences but also from failures and from countries that have made progress in PSR but that did not borrow from the Bank for this purpose. A member found that the findings of this IEG evaluation are similar to the main messages of the 1997 WDR

and of the 1999 IEG evaluation on civil service reform and wondered what the real progress in the Bank's PSR work has been. *Management explained how key findings from the 1997 WDR are being integrated into its work, such as focusing on the basics and being more realistic in PFM. As for the overall lower performance for CSA, management clarified that outcomes were poor in weaker governance environments but much stronger in those countries with a higher governance environment, as measured by the Country Policy and Institutional Assessment. Hence, the key challenge is CSA reform in weaker governance environments. IEG indicated that although the Bank is moving in the right direction in implementing the 1997 WDR recommendations, the report also highlights the need for continued efforts to strengthen support for PSR for which there is no single solution.*

Focus of Bank support for PSR

While noting the Bank's demonstrated comparative advantage in PFM, many speakers remarked on the need for a broader, comprehensive approach to PSR. A few of them cautioned about putting too much emphasis on PFM, which may detract from broader PSR efforts in other parts of the government, including service delivery (for example, health, environment, transport). Several others noted that PFM and CSA are interrelated and stressed the importance of continued support for CSA, which contributes to good governance. A few members supported a more nuanced approach in which the Bank should focus on areas of comparative advantage vis à vis other donors. They added that the Bank could still provide support for CSA, but this should depend on the country's request and readiness to address this area. *IEG noted that the report underscores the importance of the interlinkages between the different areas of PSR but also brings out the merits of more specific and opportunistic interventions where there is country ownership. Management agreed that PSR is broader than PFM and commented on Bank support to improve public service delivery. It also noted that the Bank's ability to support comprehensive reforms depends on country ownership and political commitment, and there is a need to be opportunistic and incremental in its intervention.* Responding to a question raised about the development of a new financial instrument to enable long-term support for PSR, *management said the appropriateness of existing instruments is being reviewed in the context of the president's six strategic themes.*

Governance and anticorruption (GAC)

Several speakers considered indirect approaches to be more effective in addressing GAC issues in PSR, such as simplifying processes and enhancing the robustness of systems, which would reduce opportunities for corruption. A member urged a clear articulation of the GAC agenda in PSR and noted the need for adequate diagnostic tools for GAC, as well as for assessing the fiduciary risks in the use of country systems for procurement, and social and environmental safeguards. He suggested that the CFAAs and CPARs should be adjusted to better track progress in GAC. A speaker reiterated the Development Committee's request for actionable governance indicators. *Management clarified that the CFAAs, the CPARs, the Public Expenditure and Financial Accountability and the Public Expenditure Review already assess the system's vulnerabilities, which could provide opportunities for corruption. It added that efforts are under way to identify and address cor-*

ruption risk through systematic corruption risk mapping in procurement systems.

Staff skill mix and budget resources

A few speakers sought information on availability of resources within the overall budget framework, appropriate staff skill to work on PSR, particularly CSA, and balance of staff between headquarters and country offices and between the Poverty Reduction and Economic Management Network and the Regions. *Management said a strategic staffing exercise is ongoing in the context of the GAC strategy, including for CSA.*

Other comments

A member asked how IEG ensures the independence of its evaluation, given the staff mobility between IEG and the Bank. *IEG explained that staff who have directly worked on the topic being evaluated do not take part in the evaluation.* There was a request for IEG to do an evaluation on Bank support for privatization of public firms. *IEG indicated it would consider future work on this, but cautioned that its work program in the near term was already very full.*

Jiayi Zou, Chairperson

Chapter 1

Evaluation Essentials

- The objective of this evaluation is to inform decision making about the selection of public sector reform programs based on what is likely to work.
- The scope of the evaluation is Bank support between fiscal 1999 and 2006 for country programs to enhance the rule-based operation of governments.
- The evaluation focuses primarily on the effectiveness of country programs.

City government building in Guayaquil, Ecuador. Photo © Damon P. Coppola.

Objective, Scope, and Method of Evaluation

The main objective of this Independent Evaluation Group (IEG) evaluation is to help the World Bank learn how to contribute more effectively to public sector reform (PSR) in its member countries.

Objectives and Framework

The intended audience also includes government officials and other stakeholders that want to see what lessons are available for improving project and program design and for better using the Bank's support for PSR.

In other words, the evaluation seeks to provide country directors or finance ministers with knowledge of what sort of PSR program is likely to work in their country, based on what has been learned from the 1999–2006 experiences.

Foremost, this evaluation considers the design of country programs for PSR—not only the content and sequence of reforms within the key thematic areas, but also the coordination and sequence of the overall program. Based on interviews with Bank managers and the experiences in a sample of countries, the evaluation also considers how the Bank organizes its PSR work and resources.

Support for improving the operation of the government has long been part of the Bank's work with countries. The rationale for this work has evolved and its centrality has grown. Since the late 1980s, it has become one of the most prominent items on the reform agenda, as will be detailed in chapters 2 and 3.

The attention to PSR has emerged from two considerations. First, the quality of the public sector—accountability, efficiency in service delivery, transparency, and so forth—correlates strongly with—and is thought by many to contribute to—long-term growth and poverty reduction, although causality probably runs both ways (Bates 2001; Kaufmann, Kraay, and Mastruzzi 2005; Przeworski and colleagues 2000; van de Walle 2001).

Second, the World Bank works primarily with government counterparts and intermediaries. Improving the efficiency of and public support for their work contributes to the effectiveness of the Bank's support to development, because 38 percent of total Bank lending during 1999–2006—amounting to $62 billion—went directly to budgets without project earmarks (policy reform lending, budget support, and so forth), and the majority of investment lending is executed by core government agencies.

The quality of the public sector has a strong relationship with growth and poverty reduction.

In 2000 the Bank produced and discussed with its Executive Board a strategy document—*Reforming Public Institutions and Strengthening Governance: A World Bank Strategy*.[1] The strategy aimed to help build efficient and accountable public sector institutions in addition to providing discrete policy advice. The strategy noted that a main lesson from experiences in the 1990s was that "neither good policies nor good investments are likely to emerge and be sustainable in an environment with dysfunctional institutions and poor governance" (World Bank 2000, p. vii).

The PSR strategy "focuses primarily on core public sector institutions and their interface with sectoral institutions. It touches only lightly on institutional concerns within specific sectors… and it does so primarily to point out generic issues that concern many sectors" (World Bank 2000, p. 12).

A Bank-wide strategy for PSR was published in 2000.

The strategy identified eight areas of public sector reform in which Bank activities could contribute:

- Public expenditure analysis and management
- Administrative and civil service reform
- Revenue policy and administration
- Anticorruption
- Decentralization
- Legal and judicial reform
- Sectoral institution building
- Public enterprise reform.

Concerning tactics to work in these areas, the strategy also said that PSR support should avoid trying to make "one size fit all" and should aim to ensure that basic reforms were done first, before attempting more sophisticated ones.

Scope

PSR is part of the agenda for improving governance, which includes three broad areas: rule-based operation of the government itself to improve the supply of public goods, voice and accountability for citizens to demand better public services, and more efficient and effective regulation of the private sector to improve its competitiveness.[2] PSR in this document refers mainly to the first area and to the aspects of the second that deal with transparency and access to information. It does not deal with regulation of the private sector.

To assess the relevance and effectiveness of the PSR strategy, the evaluation focuses on projects in the period between fiscal 1999 and 2006, and it also looks back to the previous decade to see

the long term of countries' PSR programs. The evaluation focuses on the four areas outlined in the Bank's 2000 public sector strategy that pertain to the way the core government organizes itself:

- ***Public financial management* (PFM)** concerns the management of money through the entire budget cycle. This includes budget planning and execution, in particular, financial management information systems and medium-term expenditure frameworks (MTEFs), procurement, auditing, and monitoring and evaluation. It also includes the implementation of reforms arising from country financial accountability assessments (CFAAs) and country procurement assessment reviews (CPARs) and the strengthening of key budgetary accountability institutions, such as public accounts committees of the legislature and supreme audit institutions.

- ***Civil service and administrative* (CSA) *reform*** involves all aspects of the management and organization of personnel. It includes programs to downsize the civil service and reforms to the personnel information system (including civil service censuses), career paths, pay grades (decompression), other aspects of the incentive system, and the organization of ministries.

- ***Tax administration reform*** includes the key aspects of revenue administration, particularly the institutional setting and development of operational processes, including automation and interaction with taxpayers (actual and potential).[3]

- ***Anticorruption and transparency* (ACT)** reforms are involved in the first three areas; going further, many recent operations support specific activities to combat corruption and improve transparency across the public sector.[4] Box 1.1 explains how the Bank support evaluated here relates to the full spectrum of work on anticorruption.

The evaluation recognizes the interdependence of these components of PSR and recognizes that the Bank's PSR programs have sometimes worked across these dimensions. This evaluation does not delve into sector-specific issues or the reform

---

Box 1.1: Scope of Review on the Bank's Anticorruption Activity

This IEG evaluation reviews only part of the World Bank's work on anticorruption, dealing with cross-cutting systems (IEG evaluated the full range of the Bank's anticorruption work in 2004; IEG 2004b). The Bank's Anticorruption Strategy, endorsed by the Board in 1997, contained four principal pillars:

- *Mainstreaming anticorruption in country analysis, country strategy, and lending decisions.* This includes the CPIA for the International Development Association resource allocation and anticorruption in country assistance strategies (for example, Indonesia, Bangladesh, and Albania).
- *Helping countries that request assistance in curbing corruption.* This includes support for cross-cutting public management systems and transparency reforms, as well as anticorruption in key sectors, such as extractive industries, health, education, and transport.
- *Preventing fraud and corruption in Bank projects and programs.* This includes fiduciary controls (financial management, procurement, risk mapping, and mitigation) and investigation of fraud and corruption by the Bank's Department of Institutional Integrity.
- *Contributing to international efforts to fight corruption.* This includes collaboration with donors, the Development Assis-

tance Committee of the Organisation for Economic Co-operation and Development (OECD), and support for regional and global conventions such as the OECD Convention against Bribery of Foreign Officials.

This review primarily covers anticorruption aspects in the second pillar, focusing on cross-cutting public management systems but not on anticorruption reforms in individual sectors.

The 2007 Governance and Anticorruption Strategy (GAC) consists of three broad levels:

(i) *Country level:* Helping countries build more capable and accountable systems (including core public management systems, demand-side institutions, and sectoral institutions)
(ii) *Project level:* Combating corruption in Bank operations
(iii) *Global level:* Global partnerships and collective action.

This IEG evaluation primarily focuses on the country level of the GAC strategy dealing with strengthening core public management systems, but covering projects and activities undertaken before the launch of the 2007 strategy. The GAC strategy has just commenced implementation, and an IEG evaluation on the GAC is planned in due course.

---

of state-owned enterprises, which are important but deserve separate treatment.

The present evaluation considers all types of Bank activities to support PSR in countries, including development policy and investment/technical assistance loans, institutional development fund (IDF) and other grants, and the major institutional pieces in all types of analytical and advisory activities (AAA), such as Public Expenditure Reviews (PERs), Institutional and Governance Reviews (IGRs), and others. Consideration of AAA has been coordinated with IEG's ongoing evaluation of economic and sector work (ESW).

The evaluation covers the period mainly from fiscal 1999 through 2006. Thus, it does not evaluate the 2007 Governance and Anticorruption (GAC) strategy, which could address some of the issues

raised in this evaluation; whether that strategy does so will depend on the implementation. The Board approved the strategy in April 2007 and the implementation plan in October 2007.

Criteria for Evaluation

In terms of IEG's three standard evaluation concerns—relevance, efficacy, and efficiency—this evaluation is mainly about efficacy, that is, seeing what the Bank-supported programs have done and figuring out what was **effective** and why.

The evaluation concurs with the public sector strategy: in essentially all the borrowing countries, the objective of PSR is **relevant**, generally and in the four areas of evaluation focus. The proper management of those resources must be a key determinant of development because core

Table 1.1: Results Framework for Public Sector Reform

Ultimate desired impacts	PSR areas and outcomes	Outputs in the countries	Inputs from the Bank's country programs
	Public expenditure and financial management Fiscal discipline, allocation of resources consistent with policy priorities, and good operational management	Comprehensive budget; transparent budget planning, approval, and execution; robust and timely accounting and audit; cost-effective and transparent procurement (CPIA 13)	
Economic growth	**Civil service and administrative reform**		Development policy lending
Reduced poverty	High-performing public service that attracts, retains, and motivates competent staff; transparent, nondiscretionary pay regime appropriate to local labor market; wage bill within budget constraint	Adequate personnel information system; reduced salary compression and turnover; adequate training; effective business processes and interministerial coordination (CPIA 15)	Technical assistance/ investment lending
Security of life and property			
Participation and empowerment of people			IDF and other grants
	Tax administration		
Improved quality of and access to public services (water, health, and so forth)	Improved revenue performance; more equitable and efficient tax system, reduced tax evasion; more open to citizen feedback	Improved information system; well-paid staff; reduced arrears; reduced cost of taxpayer compliance; reduced collection cost (CPIA 14b)	AAA (PERs, PRSPS, IGRs, other)
	Anticorruption and transparency Executive branch and personnel are held accountable for use of funds and other actions; accountability enhanced by audit institutions and public access to information; accountability and transparency help discourage use of public office for private gain	In addition to anticorruption measures in the three areas above, clear rules about conflict of interest; sanctions enforced through effective laws, audits, prosecution, and judiciary; public has access to information and protection for whistle-blowers (CPIA 16)	

Note: AAA = analytical and advisory activities; CPIA = Country Policy and Institutional Assessment; IDF = institutional development fund; IGR = Institutional and Governance Review; PER = Public Expenditure Review; PRSP = Poverty Reduction Strategy Paper.

public sector spending accounts for 15 percent to 30 percent of gross domestic product in the Bank's borrowing countries. In another view, 38 percent of total Bank financing during 1999–2006 went directly to budgets without project earmarks (development policy lending, budget support, debt relief, and so forth), and the great majority of investment lending is executed by core government agencies. Therefore, improving the core public sector is essential for the overall effectiveness of the Bank's support to development.

The World Bank's results framework for PSR in table 1.1[5] shows how PSR can contribute to the goals of poverty reduction and growth, as well as accountability of government to citizens. This evaluation takes the potential connection as a given and examines the extent to which programs achieved the objectives of PSR.

Obviously, programs are **efficient** only if they are effective. Coordination of Bank staff and donor support, or its lack, would qualify as an efficiency issue. To what extent were staff skills, internal organization, incentives, and relations with external partners aligned for effective support to the country? By and large, however, the Bank and others are still trying to figure out what works; fine tuning for efficiency can come afterward.

The question of how effectively the Bank's strategy was implemented at the country level implies several more specific questions:

- Was Bank support at the country level based on sound analysis and adequate knowledge of institutional and political realities?
- To what extent was the Bank-supported program tailored to fit the needs of the country and to take account of institutional and political realities? To what extent did the Bank use a prioritized and phased approach? Did the program address basics first?
- Which entry points for the PSR agenda worked best?
- To what extent did the Bank use lending and AAA instruments appropriate for country conditions, including the degree of reform commitment?

In assessing results, the evaluation draws lessons on whether the Bank has achieved better results in some areas of PSR than in others or whether it has generated better results in some types of country situations than in others. The question has two parts regarding to what extent the Bank contributed to PSR in client countries:

- To what extent did PSR succeed in countries where the Bank was providing support?
- What aspect of the Bank support, if any, contributed to the success?

Attributing PSR results to Bank support poses a challenge. The evidence for definitive successes generally emerges in the longer term, for which there are only preliminary conclusions. In addition to the World Bank program influences, the review considers the impact of conditions in the country and the programs of other actors, such as international finance institutions (the International Monetary Fund [IMF] and regional development banks) and bilateral donors. Important country conditions include (i) macroeconomic conditions, which are linked (causation is in both directions) to the fiscal situation of the government and therefore its ability to address long-term priorities; (ii) labor market conditions, which affect the challenges for personnel reforms in the public sector; and (iii) political conditions and events, because most authors on the subject identify political support as essential for success in PSR.

The attribution of PSR results to Bank support is difficult.

Methods

The evaluation employs three main ways to answer questions: country case analyses, thematic analyses of the four selected thematic dimensions, and statistical analysis of the pattern of

Table 1.2: Case Study Countries

Region	IDA	IBRD
Sub-Saharan Africa	Burkina Faso,[a] Ethiopia, Ghana, Sierra Leone, Tanzania,[a] Uganda	
East Asia and Pacific	Cambodia[a]	Indonesia (blend)
Europe and Central Asia	Albania	Bulgaria,[a] Russian Fed.
Latin America and the Caribbean	Bolivia, Guyana, Honduras,	Argentina, Guatemala
Middle East and North Africa	Yemen, Rep. of	
South Asia	Bangladesh	India (blend)[a]

a. Countries where the team made field visits.

PSR interventions and outcomes in the full set of countries for which data are available. The evaluation also draws on the previous IEG evaluations of public expenditure reviews (IEG 1998), civil service reform (IEG 1999), anticorruption activities (IEG 2004b), capacity building in Africa (IEG 2005), support to low-income countries under stress (IEG 2006b), and fiduciary instruments—CFAAs and CPARs (IEG 2007)—plus relevant Country Assistance Evaluations and Project Performance Audit Reports (PPARs). All aspects of the evaluation were informed by interviews with task managers and other relevant staff, field visits, and exchange with IEG teams doing country assistance evaluations and relevant PPARs.

The main unit of analysis is the country program, as it is generally recognized that success in PSR depends on a combination of support instruments, which cannot therefore be well appreciated in isolation.

Statistical analysis

For the full set of Bank borrower countries, there are three types of analysis of the pattern of public sector issues, interventions, and outcomes. First, chapter 3 examines the pattern of choices for PSR intervention, particularly how they relate to a country's International Bank for Reconstruction and Development (IBRD) or International Development Association (IDA) status and to the initial quality of the public sector in the country. Second, the chapter looks at the medium-term change in public sector quality indicators in the countries where the Bank has worked on PSR. Third, it examines the data to see what factors correlate with project success, as measured in IEG reviews of Implementation Completion Reports.

The main unit of analysis for the evaluation is the country program.

Chapter 4 looks at the evidence on these two questions, organized by country groups. It also discusses the quality of data and the questions of at-tribution. Chapter 5 examines the evidence on effectiveness according to theme.

Country analysis

With a topic as nuanced and country specific as PSR, country cases are an important complement to statistical analysis. The country reviews contributed to an understanding of how different combinations of interventions work in various country settings. The evaluation team did desk reviews of the Bank-supported programs for PSR in 19 countries, drawing on country assistance evaluation findings and PPARs, where available; for six of the analyses the team also made field visits (table 1.2).

Countries represented different Regions, subregions, and income groups, and all the countries had substantial Bank support in PSR. The selection of countries was also coordinated with the decentralization and legal/judicial evaluations to reduce the burden of the evaluations on client and Bank staff time.

Each country-level review examined the role of PSR within the country assistance strategy (CAS). Each also explored how the strategy was implemented and what contribution Bank support made to achieving the PSR objectives. The evolving economic, political, and institutional capacity conditions in each country affected the outcomes, and the evaluation considers whether the Bank took appropriate account of these conditions in the design and implementation phases of its support.

Thematic analyses

These compare the evolution of Bank practice with the state of the art in the four thematic areas. They begin with a review of the literature on international experience and then pose questions to be covered in the country studies. Then, drawing on the results of the statistical analysis and country studies, they describe the patterns of success and failure of the most common approaches in each thematic area.

Chapter 2

Evaluation Essentials

- The Bank's engagement with PSR has gone through four phases.
- PSR was initially neglected, except in building institutions to carry out public investment projects that the Bank was financing.
- In the 1980s, institutional development gained recognition as a key component for carrying out policy reforms supported by development policy lending.
- In the 1990s, many became convinced that institutional development needed to be central in most CASs.
- Since 1997, the public sector and governance agenda has been formalized, and anticorruption has been added explicitly.

The north block of the Secretariat building in Delhi, India, is the administrative heart of the government.

Photo © Patrick Horton/Lonely Planet Images.

Historical Overview of Public Sector Reform at the World Bank

The current prominence of public sector governance in the World Bank is a relatively recent feature of its agenda. Issues related to public sector capability have been present in Bank operations from its earliest days, above all when it came to evaluating creditworthiness and making decisions to lend and when ad hoc institutions were designed to ensure the success of specific projects.

Only recently, however, has the Bank identified governmental capability as a central obstacle to successful development and allocated an important share of its funding operations and analytical work to improving the institutional capability of borrowers, not only in the specific projects or sectors financed by the Bank, but in the overall conduct of government functions.

The Bank's engagement with PSR has gone through four main phases. The discussion of them is based on interviews with more than 45 current and former Bank staff and on review of more than 75 documents and publications (see Bibliography and appendix E [see http://www.worldbank.org/ieg/psr/appendix.html for appendix E]).

1946–82—PSR was neglected except in the building of institutions to carry out public investment projects that the Bank was financing.

1983–89—Institutional development gained recognition as a key component for carrying out policy reforms supported by adjustment lending.

1990–96—The collapse of communist states, frequent failures of macroeconomic adjustment programs, and persistence of project loan failures in Africa convinced many people that institutional development needed to be central in most CASs.

1997–2007—The public sector and governance agenda was formalized, and anticorruption was added explicitly to the agenda.

1946 to 1982: PSR at the Margins

During the Bank's first 36 years of operation, public sector management (PSM) capacity was almost entirely absent in Bank statements, as a major determinant either of the success of Bank projects or of overall economic development in borrower countries. Only a small number of loans and technical assistance projects concerned themselves with broad institutional development in member countries, beyond the design of specific project implementation units.

The Bank initially neglected PSR except to build up institutions to carry out investment projects that the Bank was financing.

The vigorous institutional development and PSM effort by other donors suggests that the 36-year-long, almost complete absence of that work in the Bank's agenda had more to do with particular features of the institution than with predominant development thinking. The most evident distinctive feature separating the Bank from other donors during the first two to three decades of its existence was its dependency on market financing. To raise funds in the market, the Bank cultivated a lending culture that stressed visibly and measurably productive loans, stressed the energy and transport infrastructure sectors, and downplayed social and institutional objectives. The creation of IDA in 1960 introduced a quasi-grant element into Bank lending, but Bank lending strategy remained constrained by the primacy of market funding well into the 1970s.

Among the earliest sources of contact with public administration issues were country surveys prepared by Bank missions between 1950 and 1966. In all, 25 surveys were carried out—the first in Colombia and the last in Morocco. Many touched on basic issues of administrative capabilities and political economy. Some of the reports, such as the one on Colombia, resulted in the creation of new national bodies for programming and planning or in strengthening machinery already in existence.

The Bank's initial involvement with PSM took the form of an insistence on national planning mechanisms in borrower countries (Mason and Asher 1973). The second area of institutional development in which the Bank was operationally involved was the creation of development finance institutions. Between 1950 and 1971, the Bank helped design and fund 39 such operations, mostly during the 1960s.

More broadly, the Bank was drawn increasingly into the creation, support, and guidance of project implementation units (PIUs) and sector institutions as instruments to ensure efficient management and coordination of energy, transport, and agricultural investments. The development of sector lending in particular enabled the Bank to contribute to the strengthening of government in specific areas, such as railways and communications

In the 1980s, institutional development gained recognition as a key component for carrying out policy reforms supported by adjustment lending.

in India, power in Mexico and Colombia, and ports in other countries.

Another encounter with public administration took the form of a growing volume of training and advisory work, including technical assistance missions and the creation of the Economic Development Institute in 1956—an implicit recognition of deficiencies in government capacity. By the early 1950s, there was a "growing belief at the Bank that the relatively low level of economic management in the countries which it dealt with constituted a major impediment to development" (Mason and Asher 1973, p. 324), and in 1952, the Board approved the exploration of a training initiative. Nonetheless, government managerial capacity was not a significant feature in the Bank's strategy in these years.

An exception to the prevailing neglect of government capacity during these years was a study on rural development in Africa (Lele 1975). The study contains a rich discussion of cultural factors affecting rural development and of the need "to build human and institutional development capacities." The subsequent increase in concern for good government, in both analysis and operations, came to be closely associated with the Sub-Saharan Africa Region, where extreme governmental deficiencies became the seeds for a strategic reappraisal. A subsequent study reinforced the call for attention to government capacity (World Bank 1981).

1983 to 1989: Focus on Quality of Government

Quality of government first appeared as a central developmental issue for the Bank in the 1983 World Development Report (World Bank 1983). The principal section in the report, "Management in Development," discussed the appropriate size, role, and managerial efficiency of the state:

Policy and institutional reform are complementary. Policies are relevant only if there is the institutional capacity to carry them out, while strong institutions are ineffective—even counterproductive—if the policy framework discourages efficiency (World Bank 1983).

One precipitating factor for this conceptual "bend in the road" was the strong evidence that government weakness and corruption was key to explaining the project failures and disappointing development record of the 1970s, especially in Africa. In both rich and poor countries, the previous development model had placed a great deal of faith in government, but financial crisis and economic failure naturally led to a reappraisal of government's role and capabilities.

A new consensus developed in favor of smaller and better government. In response to the Legal Department's objections against any political intervention by the Bank, the concern for governmental quality was cast in the politically neutral terms of managerial capacities.

The changing composition of Bank operations also contributed to the rethinking of government. During the 1970s the Bank expanded its work related to basic needs policies and its lending for education, health, and urban social infrastructure—sectors that demanded more of the general administrative capacities of governments than infrastructure lending. Furthermore, the rise in adjustment lending drew the attention of the Bank and policy makers to the institutional constraints on successful adjustment; policy reforms needed institutions that could implement them.

In 1983, the Bank created its first organizational unit dedicated to research and operational support related to administrative efficiency in government, the Public Sector Management Unit. During the 1980s, the unit devoted much of its time to the restructuring of public enterprises. Another line of PSM work was civil service reform, focusing especially on downsizing.

By 1986, in addition to the central PSM unit, specialized PSM units had been created in three Regional departments and in the Industrial Restructuring Division. A 1986 internal review of institutional development lending found that most

Bank managers were not convinced of the worth of institutional development work and that the Bank lacked intellectual and conceptual leadership in the institutional development field.

The growth of structural adjustment and sector adjustment lending throughout this period became a vehicle for an expansion and broadening of the scope of institutional development operations. Adjustment lending could accommodate a variety of concerns and targets, creating space for reform in core administration, especially in civil service and financial management, and for across-the-board reform in the management of state-owned enterprises.

A review of institutional development work carried out through sector adjustment loans between 1983 and 1987 found that 55 of 65 sector adjustment loans approved by the Bank included institutional development components and that results were mixed, with good implementation of simpler reforms but poor results with more complex and politically sensitive reforms (Paul 1990). Though much institutional development work was packaged in adjustment loans, the principal instrument for achieving institutional development was project-related and freestanding technical assistance, which accounted for 95 percent of total Bank technical assistance resources during the 1980s.

The growth of adjustment lending in the 1980s became a vehicle for expanding and broadening the scope of the Bank's institutional development operations.

A more complete study of PSM operations during the 1980s mirrored previous conclusions; the record was mixed. PSM successes had been limited, and roughly half the PSM effort had gone into Africa, where dramatic breakthroughs were lacking. The key problems were the political costs of bureaucratic reform and the long maturation periods required for PSM success. The relatively unsatisfactory record of institutional development efforts during these years was confirmed by a 1988 IEG review of performance evaluation, which noted that in a large number of operations the principal determinants of underperformance were institutional. A special report on Africa concluded,

"The root cause of weak performance has been the failure of public institutions" (World Bank 1989).

1990 to 1996: Increasing Awareness of Governance Agenda

Between 1990 and 1996, four factors increased the Bank's awareness of the governance agenda and induced a more active response: (i) the collapse of communism, which created an unprecedented need for reconstructing the public sector; (ii) recognition of the need for "second-generation" reforms of the institutions; (iii) donors' increasing demands and expectations for IDA as conditions for the replenishment of IDA funding; and (iv) the unacceptable failure rate of investment lending, especially in Africa. Intellectual currents also came to bear, as institutional economics helped to legitimize the governance-related concerns voiced by noneconomists.

In the 1990s, many became convinced that institutional development needed to be central in most CASs.

The operational response toward the former communist states transitioning to democracy and a market economy went through a learning process, moving from privatization and social safety support to a growing recognition of the need for core institutional and public administration development:

> *At the beginning of the transition, the Bank understood the need to reorient and strengthen public sector institutions, but it greatly underestimated the consequences of still-weak core institutions and public administrations managing the transition process . . . . PSM reform has often been approached in an ad hoc manner, without a comprehensive long-term institutional development and reform strategy* (IEG 2004a, p. viii).

The Bank's report on adjustment lending (World Bank 1990) recognized that early adjustment loans were often too optimistic about governments' implementation capacity and reform commitment. This directed attention both to measures that enhance government implementation capabilities and to what the

A 1992 task force justified Bank involvement in governance, particularly in political aspects that had previously been proscribed.

report called "the political economy of reform." In the pursuit of growth, conditionality had thus evolved to include administrative reforms as well as macroeconomic measures. Although it stated that the Bank must avoid interfering in politics, the report considered that "the cost of failure was too great for the borrowing countries and the Bank to ignore the potential contribution of a better understanding of the reality of the political economy of adjustment."

A task force report titled *Governance and Development* (World Bank 1992a) spelled out a justification for Bank involvement in matters of governance, particularly in its more sensitive, political aspects such as the rule of law, transparency, corruption, and military expenditures. It said little about the traditional "technocratic" aspects of public sector financial and human resource management; these already had a long record in the Bank's agenda, and the issues had more to do with efficacy than legal and political propriety.

The heart of the report was an elucidation of the relationship between economic growth and governance. The report ended by sanctioning particular governance considerations that had previously been excluded.

In October 1996, World Bank President James Wolfensohn set new precedents by speaking out against "the cancer of corruption" at that year's Annual Meeting (Wolfensohn 1996). This speech opened the way to a more explicit discussion of the subject within the Bank. This was made acceptable under the Bank's bylaws by redefining "the 'C' word not as a political issue but as something social and economic" (Mallaby 2004, p. 176).

There was a cost to this tactic in that the Bank would engage on the corruption issue while still, in practice, adhering to a prohibition against looking seriously at the political system, which is often the root cause of corruption (Thomas 2007, p. 742). Perhaps the biggest boost to the growing anticorruption movement came about because of the East Asian crisis of 1997–98, in which public opinion identified market failures with corruption, most notoriously in Indonesia.

1997 to 2007: PSR Efforts Become Central, Include Anticorruption

The Bank's work on broad institutional development and governance increased substantially between 1997 and 2000. This work moved to the center of CASs, as will be elaborated in the next chapter.

The 1997 World Development Report, *The State in a Changing World* (World Bank 1997b), laid out the rationale and created an official commitment for that enhanced role. In the same year, the Bank issued a report titled *Helping Countries Combat Corruption: The Role of the World Bank* (World Bank 1997a). This report stated the developmental and legal rationale for including anticorruption in the Bank's agenda; admitted that "the Bank has some catching up to do," including with its internal controls; and laid out a comprehensive operational proposal that placed anticorruption efforts within the Bank's framework for improving PSM and governance. It also highlighted cooperation with civil society and other donors.

The greater prominence of the governance theme after 1997 was more of a tipping point than a major change in the underlying forces. For a decade or more, the most powerful factor driving governance was the rising tide of democracy. This factor was most dramatic in the transition countries, but also in Latin America and, more spottily, even in some African and Middle Eastern countries. Democracy brought the rhetoric of accountability, decentralization, transparency, and rule of law, all of which relaxed the inhibitions that had previously prevented the Bank from including such topics in country dialogues with a large number of borrowers—much less incorporating them as loan conditions. A related factor was the end of the Cold War, which relaxed the pressure to support authoritarian and corrupt governments for political reasons. The Bank now had a freer hand to engage governments on governance issues.

This trend was closely related to the vigorous growth of civil society organizations and the Bank's relations with them. Nongovernmental organizations (NGOs) emerged as active development partners of governments in social and environmental work and also as watchdogs of governments. In both roles, stronger civil society was itself a major form of institutional growth and acted as advance troops for the direction in which the Bank was going.

Non-Bank donors were moving in the same direction, placing greater priority on governance and civil society in their aid programs. They not only set an example and created expertise but also influenced the Bank from within, through financial leverage of the substantial donor trust funds managed by the Bank.

Rising concerns with corruption contributed to the strategic reformulation during this period. One cause was the publication of comparative measurements of governance, including corruption, by several sources, including Transparency International. The message of these ratings was reinforced by emerging revelations of large-scale corruption in several borrower countries. The argument that corruption was only part of a larger problem changed from a reason for inaction on corruption into a reason for action across the whole governance front.

Prominence of the governance theme after 1997 was more of a tipping point than a major change in the underlying forces.

Following the publication of the 1997 World Development Report, other circumstances came into play to reinforce a governance agenda. One was a new strategic proposal, the Comprehensive Development Framework. This framework gained important momentum in 1999 when the G-7 agreed to support an enhanced Heavily Indebted Poor Countries (HIPC) Initiative. The new initiative was tightly monitored to ensure that debt relief funds would be spent honestly and applied toward poverty reduction. The Comprehensive Development Framework was aptly suited for the across-the-board surveillance and control of governance implied by the enhanced initiative.

The step from soft IDA credits to open HIPC debt-forgiveness grants also brought into the open the issue of the fungibility of the money the Bank loaned. The rationale for financial transfers continued to be growth and poverty reduction,

When the fungibility of money lent by the Bank emerged as an issue, pressure increased to ensure that recipient governments were efficiently using their entire budgets.

but, if funds were fungible, the loans could no longer be justified solely in terms of the cost benefit of specific investments or of promised policy changes.

To justify continued support, it would be necessary to assure taxpayers in donor countries that recipient governments were making honest and efficient use not only of the support received but of their entire budgets. The governance agenda, especially accountability and transparency, became both a way to improve development performance and a necessary condition for the continuation of IDA replenishments and of aid in general.

A 1997 reorganization of the Bank had a substantial effect on the Bank's capacity to expand PSR operations. One new thematic area, poverty reduction and economic management (PREM), was to carry forward the PSR agenda. Previously, PSM had been the responsibility of a small, specialized unit; after 1997 the field gained prominence and resources that allowed it to manage specialized PSM projects and influence a variety of operations in all regions. A coordinating mechanism was created around the same time—the Public Sector Board.[1] PREM quickly expanded its capacity for PSM, growing from about two dozen specialists in 1997 to around 200 by 2000, mostly in Regional units.

A strategy paper, *Reforming Public Institutions and Strengthening Governance: A World Bank Strategy* (World Bank 2000) set out the operational agenda for this new effort. It provided a road map for implementing an agenda of PSR for "core public institutions." These included the civil service as a whole, public financial management, legal and judicial reform, regulation of the private sector, and decentralization. This expanded coverage highlighted the shift from past operations, which had focused on the institutional capacity for specific projects. Corruption was to be "explicitly taken into account," and new, programmatic lending instruments, better suited to the com-

The 2000 strategy set out for the first time the Bank-wide agenda for PSR.

plexities and longer time requirements of institutional change, would be developed.

The fungibility problem was acknowledged and became an argument for heightened fiduciary safeguards.[2] Analytic work would be increased and moved upstream and would be more participatory to enhance local ownership and align with the cultural and historical specificity of institutional reform paths and political economy.

In 1998, the Bank increased the detail and importance of the governance part of the Country Performance and Institutional Assessment (CPIA). For allocations of IDA funding, the revised CPIA placed heavier weight on the quality of government management, including transparency and corruption, as well as the technical aspects of civil service and financial management, which had been in the CPIA before. This increased the leverage for the governance agenda.

The need for fiduciary control was more directly addressed in 2004 by a multiagency partnership—including the Bank, the IMF, and several bilaterals, with a secretariat housed in the Bank—that developed a performance measurement framework for Public Expenditure and Financial Accountability (PEFA). It focused mainly on financial management, with increased weight given to transparency and accountability and the downstream phases of the budget cycle. It also considered at the margin some aspects of civil service and tax administration.

Again in 1998, another opportunity for donor coordination arose, in this case between the World Bank and the European Bank for Reconstruction and Development. This coordination led to the creation of the Business Environment and Enterprise Performance Survey (BEEPS), which measures aspects of the business environment in 22 transition countries. Other new diagnostic instruments—the IGR, the Public Expenditure Tracking Survey (PETS), and the Quantitative Service Delivery Survey—evolved at the Bank in the late 1990s to complement the PER.

The governance agenda designed between 1997 and 2000 has mostly remained in place, with two additions. The first addition was upgrading the importance of "the demand side," meaning citizen participation, voice, and effective power in the conduct of government (see World Bank 2004b). Second, in 2006, the Bank prepared a reinforced governance and anticorruption strategy, "Strengthening World Bank Group Engagement on Governance and Anticorruption" (World Bank 2007c), which the Board approved in 2007. The strategy laid out seven principles:

- The Bank's work on GAC is part of the mandate to address poverty reduction, not an end in itself.
- Strategy must be country driven.
- Strategy must be adapted to country circumstances, not "one size fits all."

- Strategy requires the Bank to remain engaged even in countries with weak governance, so the poor do not "pay twice."
- The Bank will work with many stakeholders.
- The Bank will not act in isolation, but with partners.
- The Bank will work to strengthen, not bypass, country systems through stronger institutions.

The staff, Board, and governments recognized that the effect of this strategy would depend less on the broad principals than on the specifics of implementation, with emphasis on learning by doing. The Board approved a GAC implementation plan in October 2007 with the understanding that it would be a living document, evolving to reflect the lessons of experience.

Since 2000 the importance of citizen participation has been recognized and anticorruption has become a central concern for the Bank.

Chapter 3

Evaluation Essentials

- Almost all countries get some AAA for PSR.
- A large majority of IDA countries get lending for PSR, both investment lending and development policy lending.
- The IBRD countries are much more selective in taking PSR lending; some take investment lending and others take development policy lending.
- The Bank has put more staffing and resources for analytic work into PFM than into the areas of political economy and civil service (public administration).

Tanzanian Parliment Building, Dodoma, Tanzania. Photo © Shawn McCullars.

World Bank Support for Public Sector Reform

This chapter examines the patterns of the Bank's lending and non-lending support for PSR—over time, by Region, and by type of borrower—and the public sector outcomes associated with that support.

First, the overall package is considered, and then different types of ESW, lending, and other non-lending support are examined in more detail. Each country situation—and the Bank's response to it—is unique, yet there are some trends and patterns.

Lending Projects for Public Sector Reform

Aggregate trends

The Bank approved 467 lending projects from 1990 to 2006 with significant PSR components in the areas evaluated in this report (see figure 3.1).[1] These projects represent 11 percent of all World Bank (IBRD and IDA) loans approved over the period. Of the projects, 62 percent were development policy loans (DPLs) or credits, and the rest were investment loans. IDA financed 305 of the projects fully and 12 in part (blend financing). About two-thirds of these loans (304) have been made since 1999, and the analysis concentrates on those.

The majority of the 467 PSR projects were not categorized under ("pathed to") public sector governance (PSG), which reflects the prevalence of DPLs with PSR components that are managed by other sectors, especially economic policy. [2] The public governance sector managed about a third[3] of development policy projects with significant PSR components from 1998 to 2006. In contrast, more than three-fourths of investment loans with significant PSG components have been categorized under PSG since the mid-1990s.

Total funding to these 467 projects represents about $47 billion in commitments, or about 13 percent of Bank project lending over the period. Many of these projects contain a variety of non-PSR-related components; only 14 percent funded PSR activities exclusively.[4]

Considering only the fraction of each project (43 percent, on average) associated with PSR (see appendix A), these 467 projects represent about $20 billion (about 5.4 percent of Bank lending) in commitments designated specifically for PSR[5] (figure 3.2). About 83 percent of this funding was from DPLs. The number of DPLs (289) represented 62 percent of the 467 projects. Whereas the majority of these PSR projects were IDA agreements, more than half of the commitment amounts had IBRD funding.

Both the number and funding of PSR-related projects have risen over the last two decades. In particular, there have been significantly higher levels of PSR lending since about fiscal 2000. There was an average of 19 PSR programs per year from 1990 to 1999, but this number more than doubled to 40 programs per year from 2000 to 2006. Projects with a significant PSR component almost doubled, from 7.6 percent of Bank projects to 14.5 percent,[6] which reflects trends in Bank thinking.[7] The value of PSR lending, measured as a percentage of total Bank lending, increased sharply around 2000, from 2.6 percent of

The 467 projects represent about $20 billion in commitments designated for PSR.

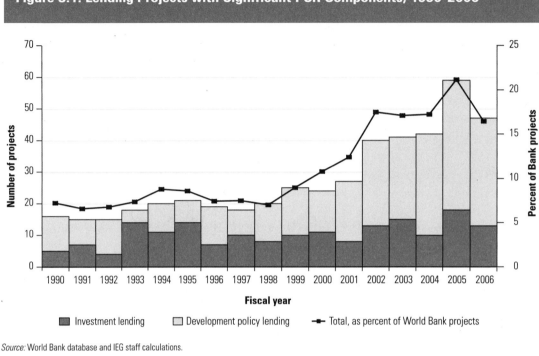

Figure 3.1: Lending Projects with Significant PSR Components, 1990–2006

Source: World Bank database and IEG staff calculations.

Bank loans in 1990–99 to 10.2 percent of lending in 2000–06.

Although development policy lending for PSR has grown steeply since 2001, the number of investment loans with significant PSR components peaked in 1993–95 (at 12–14 projects per year) and has been at or below that rate since. In other words, this mechanism for sustaining medium-term support for institutional development has not grown apace with the other means for PSR support.

The number and funding of PSR-related projects have been rising, much of the recent increase coming from policy lending related to PSR. The number of DPLs with significant PSR components did not grow rapidly until about fiscal 2001. Since then, they have predominated, partly because of the expansion of Poverty-Reduction Support Credits (PRSCs). Sometimes, and for some parts of PSR, technical assistance loans accompany the PRSCs, but in other cases the country strategy anticipated that general budget support would provide adequate incentives and resources for institutional development. At least in the cases investigated in detail,

such as Honduras, Tanzania, and Uganda, this did not happen reliably. The budget-support projects gave incentives to put resources toward big-budget, front-line, poverty-reduction sectors such as education and health but not to the smaller, back-office, institutional development for PSR. So investment PSR projects had value added in getting attention and resources to the institutional reforms, according to Bank and government sources.

Regional distribution

PSR projects were geographically concentrated in Sub-Saharan Africa (173), Latin America and the Caribbean (103), and Europe and Central Asia (90). The number of projects increased in all Regions throughout the last 20 years, although the pace of growth varied (figure 3.3). Africa has the highest share of PSR projects throughout the period (about 15 percent of projects in the Region had significant PSR components), followed by Latin America and the Caribbean and Europe and Central Asia. South Asia had relatively few PSR projects in the 1990s; it has had 33 PSR projects since 2000, making it the second most active Region recently.

Figure 3.2: Lending Value in Projects with a Significant PSR Component

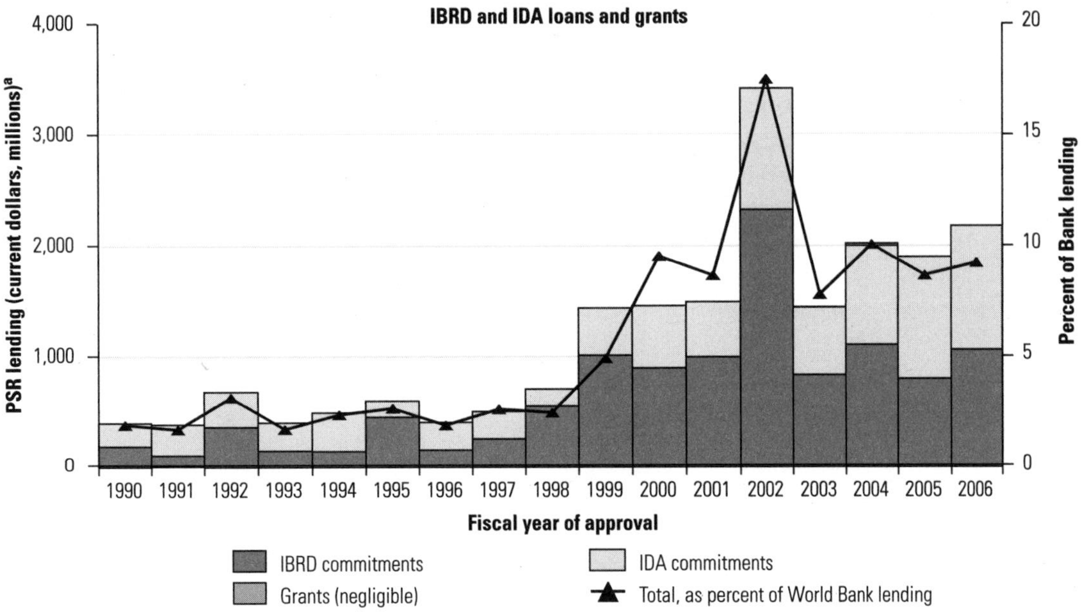

IBRD and IDA loans and grants

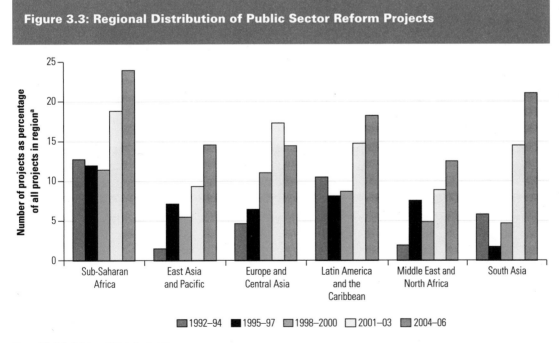

Fiscal year of approval

■ IBRD commitments ☐ IDA commitments
■ Grants (negligible) ▲ Total, as percent of World Bank lending

Source: World Bank data and IEG staff calculations.

a. The graph represents the sum of loans and grants for all projects multiplied by the share that each project allocated to a PSR theme.

Figure 3.3: Regional Distribution of Public Sector Reform Projects

■ 1992–94 ■ 1995–97 ■ 1998–2000 ☐ 2001–03 ■ 2004–06

Source: World Bank data and IEG staff calculations.

a. The graph represents numbers of projects with significant PSR components, as a percentage of all projects in the Region.

AAA Tasks for Public Sector Reform[8]

In 1999, the Bank committed to deliver for every active borrower a set of five core diagnostics: a poverty assessment, a Country Economic Memorandum (CEM)/Development Policy Review, a PER, a CPAR, and a CFAA.[9] The pace accelerated in 2001 when the Bank sought to have an up-to-date core diagnostic (less than five years old) for all active countries. The requirement was removed in 2004 because it became obvious that core diagnostic requirements were driven by Bank-specified timetables and not by the borrowers' needs.

Coverage of PSR-related AAA has increased for IDA countries.

As a result of the Bank's changing policy, as well as the increased coverage, the number of CFAAs, CPARs, and PERs peaked between 2002 and 2004 (see table 3.1). After a sharp decline in the number of CEMs in 2001, the number increased again in 2003 and has remained stable since. The number of IGRs has steadily increased in the past four years (appendix C [http://www.worldbank.org/ieg/psr.appendix.html] has a list of AAA on PSR).

Coverage of AAA for IDA countries has increased. At the end of fiscal 2006, 54 percent of active IDA-eligible countries were covered with up-to-date (five years or less) core diagnostic products, compared with only 13 percent at the end of fiscal 2003. About 85 percent of these had an up-to-date fiduciary study at the end of fiscal 2006, compared with only 46 percent three years earlier. Analytical work in fragile states has significantly increased since 2001: More than 85 percent have up-to-date PERs and CFAAs; roughly 80 percent have CPARs; more than half have a recent poverty assessment, and more than one-third have a CEM/Development Policy Review. The Bank also

Table 3.1: Public Sector Reform AAA Products (number of products)

	Fiscal 1999–2000	Fiscal 2001–02	Fiscal 2003–04	Fiscal 2005–06	Total
Core ESW	**41**	**111**	**198**	**124**	**474**
Fiduciary studies[a]	14	66	104	44	228
PSR CEM/Development Policy Review[b]	12	14	46	40	112
PSR Public Expenditure Review[b]	15	31	48	40	134
Noncore products					
ESW	**42**	**46**	**43**	**67**	**198**
Public financial management	13	18	16	39	86
Tax administration	1	0	0	1	2
Civil service and administration	8	9	8	6	31
Anticorruption and transparency	20	19	19	21	79
of which: IGRs	0	3	5	10	18
Nonlending technical assistance	**15**	**25**	**41**	**50**	**131**
Public financial management	4	10	18	34	66
Tax administration	0	2	2	1	5
Civil service and administration	1	2	9	10	22
Anticorruption and transparency	10	11	12	5	38
Total, core and noncore	**98**	**182**	**282**	**241**	**803**

Source: World Bank data and IEG staff calculations.

Note: AAA = analytical and advisory activities; CEM = Country Economic Memorandum; ESW = economic and sector work; IGRs = Institutional Governance Reviews; PSR = public sector reform.

a. Country Financial Accountability Assessment, Country Procurement Assessment, and Integrative Fiduciary Assessment.

b. Reports that had as main two sectors the following sectors: general public administration, central government administration, PSM, PFM, civil service reform, other PSR, institutional development, and subnational government.

nearly doubled the budget for AAA in low-income countries under stress during fiscal 2003–05 compared with fiscal 2000–02.

PERs have the longest history of AAA in addressing PSR issues, along with macrofiscal and sectoral concerns. Since 1999 there have been 161 PERs, with at least one in 72 percent of borrower countries. More than three-fourths of PERs since the late 1990s have given substantial attention to PSR, typically with chapters on the process of formulating and (more recently) executing the budget.

A forthcoming IEG review of AAA finds that PERs have substantial positive effect, especially programmatic ones that are becoming more common. In some cases, PERs have become part of the regular budget cycle and thus contribute to the PFM capacity building, even if there is not an explicit section on institutions.

For instance, in Tanzania, a good PER with substantive institutional analysis led the government to decide to do a PER every year and to have a public conference on the report every year to launch its budget discussions. The PERs discuss how well the execution of the budget matched what was approved by parliament the year before and lay out options for the future composition of spending. Donors participate in this conference, and it has become a focal point for their decisions about what aid to pledge in support of the budget.

Fiduciary studies, CFAAs, and CPARs are now the most widespread form of AAA—79 percent of countries have at least one—and are often done in conjunction with PERs. IEG's evaluation of the instrument (IEG 2007) found that CFAAs have shown steady improvement in quality since guidelines were issued in 2003, increasing from 27 percent satisfactory (including moderately satisfactory) in fiscal 2001 to 97 percent in fiscal 2004 and 2005. For CPARs, the average quality of reports before the 2002 guidelines was 49 percent satisfactory; this increased to 84 percent satisfactory between fiscal 2003 and 2005.

Nonetheless, action plans often lack an appropriately phased approach. Client consultation in the preparation of CFAAs and CPARs has increased, but the three Bank units dealing with PFM have often not coordinated adequately, resulting in fragmented action plans for clients.

Although core diagnostics added coherence to overall country AAA, in small countries they sometimes crowded out other AAA for PSR that might have had better value.

Fiduciary studies have been done in 79 percent of countries, but even with improving quality, many still result in fragmented action plans.

Institutional Development Grants

IDF grants concentrate on PSR. The IDFs, established in fiscal 1993, support capacity building and are part of nonlending technical assistance. IDF grants are relatively small and last no more than three years.[10] A 2001 review recommended that the IDF "focus its grants more sharply, particularly on governance," and identified two focus areas: financial accountability (financial management and procurement) and legal and judicial systems (World Bank 2001).

Most IDF grants are concentrated in the area of PSG (table 3.2): in public expenditure and financial accountability (44 percent in fiscal 2004, 34 percent in fiscal 2005), in monitoring and evaluation (16 percent in fiscal 2004 and 22 percent in fiscal 2005), and in procurement (10 percent in fiscal 2004, 18 percent in fiscal 2005). Civil service, on the other hand, has a low and static number of IDFs.

Country Portfolios of PSR Activities

Overall improvement to PSM requires achievements in all thematic areas, which the Bank can and often does support in multiple ways. The success of PSR in a country therefore depends on the package of activities that the Bank and other multilateral and bilateral organizations support. In the country case studies (further discussed in chapters 4 and 5), the evaluation considers the overall donor package. This chapter considers how the package of Bank support for PSR—lending and AAA—varies across countries and in different situations.

Table 3.3 shows how the pattern of Bank activities—PSR investment and DPLs/credits and AAA—

Table 3.2: IDF Grants on Public Sector Reform Themes (numbers of grants)

PSR theme	Fiscal 1995–98	Fiscal 1999–2002	Fiscal 2003–06	Total
Public financial management	38	37	110	185
Tax administration	3	2	1	6
Civil service and administration	21	8	12	41
Anticorruption and governance	4	14	6	24
Total	66	61	129	256

Source: World Bank data and IEG calculations.
Note: IDF = institutional development funds; PSR = public sector reform.

varies according to the borrowing window (IBRD, blend, IDA) and to the initial (1999) CPIA (13–16) governance rating as well as the change in the rating until 2006.

PSR lending has nearly always been accompanied by PSR advisory work in recent years. In contrast, that AAA was frequently unaccompanied by any significant PSR lending. From fiscal 1999 through 2006, 45 countries received PSR-related AAA without any PSR lending, but only one country received PSR lending without any PSR advisory services. For the countries that had both, AAA tasks were more frequent; only three countries had more loans than AAA.

IDFs are mostly for PSR but are less common than PFR lending in support. Of counties with PSR lending support, 43 had no IDFs for PSR, and only a few had more IDFs than loans for PSR. Fourteen countries had an IDF without any lending. Unlike with AAA, there is no reason IDFs should accompany lending, as they are intended only for agencies that are *not* getting support from lending operations. Interviews in case study countries indicated that country commitment tended to be stronger with a loan than with an IDF grant.

Table 3.3: Public Sector Reform Lending and AAA Activities in Relation to Public Sector Governance

Lending category and governance CPIA score in 1999	Percent with any PSR lending project	Percent with PSR investment project	Percent with PSR development policy project	Percent with PSR AAA task	Percent with PSR IDF	Number of countries in row (of table)
IBRD—all	47	32	40	82	49	54
4 +	27	20	13	73	47	11
3–3.9	57	32	57	86	57	28
< 3	50	43	36	86	36	15
IDA and blend—all	74	54	65	94	64	80
4 +	50	0	50	100	50	2
3–3.9	79	55	71	95	69	42
< 3	69	56	58	92	58	36

Source: World Bank data and IEG staff calculations.
Note: CPIA governance score is the average of CPIA 13–16. Countries are separated by their classification in 1999 as an IBRD, IDA, or blend country. Development policy and investment loans include those with the approval date in fiscal 1999–2006. If there is no 1999 CPIA score, the score from 2000 or 2001 is used.
AAA = analytical and advisory activities; IBRD = International Bank for Reconstruction and Development; IDA = International Development Association; IDF = institutional development funds; PSR = public sector reform.

IBRD lending

Among IBRD borrowers, governments have wide scope for selecting areas for which to borrow or to have AAA. The pattern of Bank involvement differs according to each country's initial governance situation.

Countries with initial governance CPIA ratings of 4.0 or above (11 countries) had no or, at most, one project (3 cases) in the PSR area. All but one had at least one and usually several AAA activities (ESW or nonlending technical assistance). This indicates that they no longer perceive much need for Bank PSR lending, but the governments still put at least some value in the Bank's advice on PSR via AAA.[11] Case studies verified this.

Almost all countries with an initial governance CPIA score between 3.0 and 3.9 had AAA in the PSR areas, but the lending activity varied widely: one-third had none, and almost half had two or more loans. It appears, therefore, that the PSR advice has some value for all countries, but the governments have divergent views about the usefulness of Bank lending for PSR. (Presumably it was available to virtually all of them if they wanted it. Some received support from other agencies as well or instead.)

Half of IBRD countries with poor initial governance—with scores below 3.0—asked for and received PSR lending, usually two or more loans, and all but one of the borrowers improved their governance CPIA at least 0.5 points. Therefore, it appears that (i) the Bank often did stay engaged with these problem governance states, (ii) it often did so with lending (if countries wanted it), and (iii) the engagement was usually associated with improvement in the public sector dimensions measured by the CPIA.

IDA financing

Of countries with access to IDA or blend resources,[12] three-fourths took PSR lending (credits) and almost all had AAA activities, usually numerous. Forty-eight of the countries had two or more PSR loans. These countries usually took both policy-based and investment lending, including technical assistance. IDA countries are,

therefore, more likely than mid-range IBRD countries to take PSR lending. This could reflect both a greater need in these countries for PSR and stronger pressure from the Bank and other donors to make reforms.[13]

For the 39 IDA-blend countries with initial governance CPIAs below 3.0, a larger share of cases (28) had PSR lending, and all but four had some PSR AAA. In almost all the cases with lending, the governance CPIA improved (to above 3.0 about half the time).[14] Even IDA states with relatively good initial governance (CPIA scores above 3.5) received PSR lending in five of seven cases, often multiple loans.

Of the six IDA-blend countries with Standard & Poor's credit scores in 1999 (which presumably indicated at least some credit access via the private sector), all received PSR subsequent loans; all but one received at least one DPL for PSR, and two (Pakistan and India) borrowed heavily for PSR. All six experienced improvements in their CPIA governance score from 1999 to 2006, showing the benefits of undertaking PSR reforms when the country is not desperate for funds.

If having poor public sector institutions is one of the main reasons that countries have income low enough to qualify for IDA (as many now believe), then it is appropriate and relevant that the Bank had PSR activities in virtually all these countries.[15] Global governance performance and indicators usually take longer to improve, but on the narrower measures of most CPIA governance dimensions, there was at least some improvement in the majority of cases.

Recovering postconflict states typically got substantial amounts of PSR lending and AAA. The typically strong improvement in CPIA ratings for these countries presumably reflects a combination of benefits from Bank (and other donor) support and spontaneous rebounding when a development-oriented government takes over. Some very small states, mostly islands in the

IBRD borrowers that most needed lending for PSR— those with low CPIA governance ratings— often did borrow, and the engagement usually brought improvement in public sector dimensions measured by the CPIA.

Most of the countries that did borrow for PSR improved their CPIA governance ratings.

Pacific and eastern Caribbean, got little or no lending or AAA in the PSR area. But countries that demonstrated clear disregard for good governance usually still had some AAA for PSR, although they received little or no lending.

Thematic Distribution of PSR Projects

For each PSR project, it is possible to identify whether it has components related to the four themes of PSR: PFM, CSA, tax administration (TAX), and ACT (see appendix A).

Public financial management reform

PFM was by far the most common theme: it was a major component of 81 percent (379) of the PSR projects in the data set. Although 13–14 projects per year contained PFM components in the late 1980s and 1990s, this figure has risen to more than 30 projects per year since 2000 (see figure 3.4). Many of these projects contained PFM as a primary theme of the project.[16] Although PFM investment lending has increased somewhat, DPLs with PFM components have risen the fastest since 2000.

If one multiplies the commitment amount of each loan by the share designated as a PFM theme, the amount we can attribute to PFM lending in the 467 projects with significant PSR components in-

creased from an average of $126.9 million in 1990–99 to $912.0 million per year in 2000–06. This represented an increase from 0.6 percent to 4.7 percent of total Bank lending. Institutional development grants for PFM also increased strongly, from 15 in 1992–99 to 90 in 2000–06, rising from 3 percent to 18 percent of the total number of IDF grants.

Since 1990, there has been an increase in total Bank support to PFM (including procurement); within this, there has been an increase in program lending. The number of projects with PFM components of 25 percent or greater increased from 59 over the period 1990–99 to 157 over the period 2000–06. About 31 percent of these PFM loans were DPLs in 1990–99, and this increased to about 67 percent during the years 2000–06.[17] The increased lending was supported by IDF grants for PFM, which increased from 15 in 1992–99 to 90 in 2000–06, and from 3 percent to 18 percent of the total number of IDF grants.

Loan commitments on projects with PFM components of 25 percent or greater increased from $2,179 million over the period 1990–99 to $14,946 million over the period 2000–06.

The number of PFM-focused projects (at least 25 percent of the projects) rose in all Regions from 1990–99 to 2000–06, including an increase from 22 to 64 projects in Africa, from 5 to 18 projects in East Asia and the Pacific, and from 11 to 22 projects in Europe and Central Asia. Total commitments on projects with PFM components over 25 percent rose in all Regions, most notably in Africa, Europe and Central Asia, and Latin America and the Caribbean. A World Bank review (2006g) found that 32 of 34 recent development policy operations had conditions, triggers; milestones linked to PFM-related analytic work and in most cases were appropriately sequenced, took into account parallel actions, supported the evaluation of results, and avoided addressing too many issues.

The World Bank Institute (WBI) and the Financial Management network (under Operations Policy and Country Services [OPCS]) have provided considerable nonlending technical assistance to pub-

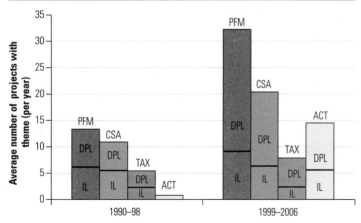

Figure 3.4: Themes Included in Projects with Significant PSR Funding

Source: World Bank database and IEG staff calculations.

Note: ACT = anticorruption and governance (transparency); CSA = civil service and administrative; DPL = development policy loan; IL = investment loan; PFM = public financial management; TAX = tax administration.

lic accounts committees and supreme audit institutions, which typically report to legislatures. This part of the budget cycle rarely gets attention in the lending process, because lending usually goes to the executive branch, so the nonlending route has been important. The WBI, for instance, has had multiyear programs in the Dominican Republic, Ghana, Guatemala, Indonesia, Nigeria, Pakistan, Senegal, Sri Lanka, Thailand, and Vietnam. Other donors, such as the United Nations Development Programme and the Canadian International Development Agency, have also been active in these areas and often look to the Bank for leadership.

The Bank has, of course, used conditionality extensively with DPLs to encourage PSR. As shown in figure 3.5, there was a recent rapid expansion in the number of legally binding conditions related to PSR.[18] This occurred even as the total number of conditions per loan declined (World Bank 2007a). This meant that the share of PSR in conditionality increased even more sharply.

The boom in PFM conditionality in 2001 reflects the growth of PRSCs and other budget-support lending, in which the expected positive effect on poverty depends on improving the country's institutions to manage the budget funds. The efficacy of this strategy to reduce poverty is being evaluated, but evidence (see chapter 5) indicates some success in the intermediate step of improving PFM.

Civil service and administration reform

CSA reform was the second most prevalent theme in PSR lending: more than half (261) of the projects with significant PSR components included a CSA theme, a measure that remained roughly constant (unlike other themes). Consistent with the overall rise in the number of projects with significant PSR components, there was an increase from about 10 projects per year with CSA components to about 20 projects per year.

The number of projects with CSA components declined in Africa (where they had been very common) and, on average, rose in all the other Regions. Like PFM, the majority of the CSA projects were DPLs.[19] The number of CSA investment

loans overall trended downward throughout the 1990s and early in this decade.

In 2002, however, there was a sudden and large increase in CSA lending, mostly with DPLs. If the commitment amount of each loan is multiplied by the share designated as a CSA theme, the amount that can be attributed to CSA lending rose from $126 million per year in 1990–99 to $422 million per year in 2000–06. This represents an increase from 0.54 percent to 2.17 percent of total Bank lending. Institutional development grants for CSA increased from 17 per year in 1992–99 to 34 in 2000–06. This represents about 35 percent of IDF grants over the entire period.

Looking at other measures of the Bank's activity in CSA generally, the number of projects with significant PSR components has grown over time, particularly since 2000. This trend reflects an increasing number of PSR projects overall, rather

Public financial management was the most common theme in PSR projects and has increased sharply since the 1990s.

More than half of projects with PSR components addressed CSA reform, mostly through development policy lending.

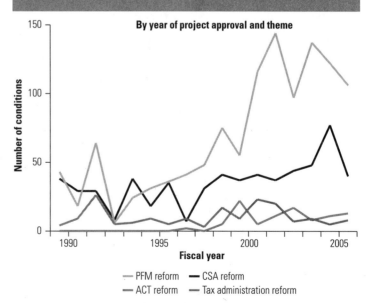

Figure 3.5: Public Sector Reform Conditions

By year of project approval and theme

(y-axis: Number of conditions, 0 to 150; x-axis: Fiscal year, 1990 to 2005)

— PFM reform   — CSA reform
— ACT reform   — Tax administration reform

Source: Adjustment Lending Conditionality and Implementation Database and IEG staff calculations.
Note: ACT = anticorruption and governance (trqansparency); CSA = civil service and administrative; PFM = public financial management.

than a greater share of projects with a CSA component, which has stayed roughly constant. This trend contrasts with both the ACT and PFM themes, where the share of projects with these components has gone up significantly over the same period (see figure 3.5).

The mix of lending instruments between investment loans (or credits) and DPLs has fluctuated since 1990. The number of investment loans with CSA content declined gradually through most of the 1990s but has risen since 2001. The number of DPLs with CSA conditions increased substantially since 2004 (figure 3.5).[20]

The case studies show that technical assistance funded with investment loans has been a particularly important tool for encouraging reform in the area of civil service reform, especially in poorer countries where capacity levels are usually very low. In some cases, the lack of supporting technical assistance was cited as a hindrance to progress where only DPLs supported CSA reform. Learning from such experiences, especially in PRSC countries, led in some cases (for example, Tanzania) to the revival of investment lending to support civil service reforms.

Tax administration reform

TAX reform was included in 24 percent of the projects with significant PSR components. It was included in almost six projects per year from 1990 to 1999 and in seven to eight projects per year from 2000 to 2006. Two-thirds of these projects were DPLs. Tax administration conditions were relatively less common overall, with only 192 legally binding conditions, roughly 27 per year from 2000 to 2006. The strong role of the IMF on tax issues may account for this. In investment projects, TAX was often the sole focus (10 percent of the investment loans with significant PSR components).

In 1999, the prevalence of anticorruption and governance reform components increased sharply.

Anticorruption and transparency reform

Project components explicitly identified as ACT reform became much more prevalent starting around fiscal 1999. Anticorruption and governance components typically supported anticorruption commissions or laws.

The term "governance" has many meanings—including legal and regulatory reform, public enterprises, public financial management, civil service, and administration of sector programs—but in the context of classifying project components, the term has usually meant transparency measures that would help reduce corruption and promote better accountability. This includes freedom of information laws and agencies. So in this evaluation, the category is called anticorruption and transparency.[21]

ACT components appeared in only nine percent of the PSR projects during the years 1990–99. From 2000 to 2006, however, 38 percent of PSR projects contained identifiable ACT components (an increase from 1.7 to 15.1 projects per year between these respective periods), mainly due to the presence of ACT conditions in policy reform projects. Increases in this indicator occurred in all Regions.

The number of projects with ACT components remains lower than the number of projects with CSA and PFM components. The number is, however, much higher than in the 1980s and 1990s, when almost no projects had ACT components. ACT does not appear to be crowding out other PSR themes. Rather, it appears that the other three themes are included in about the same fraction of PSR projects as earlier, and ACT should be understood as an addition to the typical package.[22]

Staffing for PSR

Staffing is another indicator of Bank inputs, for not all work shows up as coded activity with clear attributes. Based on a survey of Regional public sector managers, table 3.4 shows the allocation of staffing across the Regions and thematic areas.

Within in the public sector part of PREM there are almost 100 staff and regular consultants working on country support in the four areas of this evaluation's focus (not counting legal and judicial, de-

Table 3.4: Public Sector Staffing and Specialties by Region

	Total	Sub-Saharan Africa	East Asia and Pacific	Europe and Central Asia	Latin America and the Caribbean	Middle East and North Africa	South Asia
PREM	99	24	12	18	16	13	16
Public expenditure/ financial management	60	11	7	7	12	7	16
Civil service	28	9	2	6	2	3	6
Tax administration	5	0	0	4	1	0	0
Anticorruption	13	2	0	3	1	2	5
Political analysis	15	2	4	1	1	1	6
Level E/F	24	6	3	4	7	3	1
Level G	60	16	7	11	7	8	11
Level H	15	2	2	3	2	2	4
OPCS							
Financial management	33	6	5	6	5	2	9
Procurement	78	16	17	14	7	9	15

Source: IEG survey and calculations.

Note: Some people work on more than one theme, so the total of people by themes exceeds the total number of people at various personnel grade levels. The procurement figures are all the G and H level; for staff at these levels, work on the country systems is a more substantial part of their activity (rather than just procurement for Bank financed projects). PREM = Poverty Reduction and Economic Management Network; OPCS = Operations and Policy Country Services.

centralization, and so forth), plus the OPCS staff working on country systems for financial management and procurement and the PREM Economic Policy staff working on public expenditure. The Regional distribution is roughly in proportion with the distribution of projects, with the largest number in Africa, followed by Europe and Central Asia, Latin America and the Caribbean, and South Asia.

PFM specialists account for more than half of PREM staff, and there is an even larger contingent within OPCS (not counting those who mainly do financial management and procurement for Bank projects). About one-fourth of PREM public sector staff specialize in civil service. The rest specialize in tax administration or anticorruption and political analysis, plus some in decentralization and legal/judicial; those themes, however, are not the focus here. The civil service contingent is almost as large as the PFM part of PREM in Sub-Saharan Africa and Europe and Central Asia, but is much smaller in the other Regions. Tax administration specialists are all in Europe and Central Asia or Latin America and the Caribbean, with none in other Regions, despite the success of such projects in IDA countries (discussed in chapter 4).

The majority of staff are at G level, half of that E/F, and again half of that at H. The share of H-level staff in Africa was smaller than the average for the other Regions.

Although anticorruption components have grown since the 1980s, this does not appear to be crowding out other themes.

Chapter 4

Evaluation Essentials

- The majority of countries that borrowed to support reform of the core public sector had improved performance in at least some dimensions, with outliers in every category.
- IBRD countries improved more often than IDA countries, but the differences with nonborrowers were similar.
- IDA countries that had more PSR loans did better—about as well as the IBRD borrowers (one-timers)—whereas IBRD repeat borrowers did not do better.
- IEG ratings of outcome and Bank performance were also better for IBRD countries.
- Greater selectivity by countries in taking PSR loans could explain some of the difference, but IBRD would probably have better outcomes even without the selectivity effect.

Government building in Sofia, Bulgaria. Photo © J. Kaman/Travel-Images.com.

How Public Sector Reform Outcomes Differ by Country Groups

W hen governance changes in a country, it is never possible to say precisely who is responsible—who should take credit for improvement or blame for deterioration. Of course the country itself, especially the government, has the most control and responsibility, but the degree of that control varies, as does the degree of coherence within the public sector. There is never success in PSR without favorable government involvement.

Measurement, Attribution, and the Role of Governments, the Bank, and Donors

External actors come into play, including the World Bank along with other international institutions (IMF, the European Union, the United Nations Development Programme, regional development banks) and bilateral agencies. Several of them are usually involved, in close collaboration with the government when there is success, but even excellent external support alone is insufficient to guarantee success.

Measurement and timing further compound attribution. Measurements of the initial governance situation and the subsequent changes are far from perfect, even with the many improvements over the last decade. And when there is some reform effort, the effects become evident only with a lag, and an even longer lag is required to know if the effect is sustained.

Although the evidence has weaknesses, and although attribution will always be a problem, it is important to examine available evidence to con-

sider midcourse corrections if the evidence seems strong enough to suggest them.

Coordination with other donors in PSR support has gotten increasingly sophisticated and generally well adapted to the country situation. For instance, in Guyana the Inter-American Development Bank is able to do policy-based lending to complement the technical assistance work of the Bank; in Bangladesh and Indian states, the World Bank's policy-based lending complements the technical assistance grants of the United Kingdom's Department for International Development (DFID) programs. With Indian states, the Asian Development Bank and World Bank have a geographic division of labor. In Tanzania, there is now basket funding for several dimensions of PSR, to which the Bank contributes but which does not always take the lead role. The government has taken the lead, rightly insisting on better coordination. Deputy Minister Lyimo, the Bank's lead counterpart and recipient of the 2006 Gill Award, demanded of all the donors, "One process—one assessment."

Both the need for strong government participation and ownership in successful PSR and the typical participation of many donors make it difficult to have any clear attribution of results to the Bank's intervention. This is unavoidable and appropriate. What the Bank can ask for is that the process in a country to which it contributes has an impact that improves the public sector's accountability and efficiency in furthering growth and poverty reduction.

Two available measures of outcome are changes in CPIA governance indicators and IEG project ratings.

Two kinds of outcome measures are available for essentially all the countries receiving the Bank's lending projects for PSR: the changes in governance indicators and IEG project ratings. There is also less systematic but deeper information for a few counties in the case studies.

Governance measures

The CPIA is the main governance indicator considered here, though it has pros and cons (box 4.1). Indeed, one may consider the relevant CPIA indicators as the specific objectives of core PSR.[1] To measure changes in PSG, the analysis below uses the change of the average of CPIA indicators 13–16 (the governance CPIA) between 1999 and 2006.[2]

The outcomes of PSR are inherently difficult to measure. The discussion that follows provides indicative information at best. The results here indicate correlation, not causation, for several reasons:

- Imperfect measures of governance quality and the absence of these measures across wide ranges of countries and for a long enough time frame to see the effects of PSR

Box 4.1: Pros and Cons of CPIA as a Governance Measure

For this evaluation, two major advantages of the CPIA are that it covers essentially all borrower countries and that it rates performance categories that correspond closely to the thematic areas of the evaluation.

Bank staff make the CPIA ratings, so one must ask if this biases the ratings so as to invalidate them as a measure for this evaluation. Bank management uses the CPIA ratings to allocate budget and lending resources, especially for IDA countries, and wants them to be unbiased. An extensive benchmarking and vetting process is used to avoid bias and to counterbalance the natural tendency of country teams to make their countries look better. An external review of the CPIA in 2004 concluded that there was no serious bias (World Bank 2004a). Collier (2007) also uses the CPIA to define his category of failing states.

The team for this evaluation also tested whether more lending for a country biased its CPIA rating upward. (If there were such a bias, it would undermine the CPIA as an indicator of progress for countries that received lending for PSR.) For this test, we used the International Country Risk Guide (ICRG), one of the major external rating projects, with coverage similar to CPIA; its ratings are pos-

itively but not perfectly correlated with CPIA ratings. We ran a regression to see if a variable for past Bank lending explained the divergence between the two ratings. Although the coefficient on lending was statistically significant, it was very small—having another loan of any type increased the total CPIA by less than 0.02, on a scale of 1–6, compared with what the ICRG would predict. So for comparing groups of countries, the conclusion was that the CPIA was useable as a measure of initial conditions, and the change could measure the progress in PSR.

To interpret the results with the CPIA, one must bear in mind that the nature of progress measured by the CPIA (at least for the public sector items) evolves as one moves up the scale. The low ratings mostly refer to basic processes in areas of concern—such as having a publicly approved budget, having rules for hiring personnel and against accepting bribes, and having nominal rules for checks on executive authority. These are necessary steps to improving the public sector, but effective implementation and enforcement of rules to assure results only comes at the higher ratings. So a *3* is better than a *1* or *2*, but a citizen may not perceive any better services and accountability until the rating gets to *4* or *5*.

- The coarseness of most governance measures, in addition to uncertainty and imprecision
- Difficulty in capturing the timing of the impacts of the programs
- Nonrandom selection of countries for having PFM lending programs and governance ratings
- Omitted variable biases and the lack of information about PFM reforms with non-Bank sources of support.

Summary Results

Three-quarters of countries getting Bank PSR lending in the period 1999–2006 experienced at least some improvement in the governance CPIA measure. In a quarter of the cases, the improvement averaged at least one notch (0.5) across all four categories, which is substantial for the relatively short period covered. Countries with PSR lending improved 0.3 points on average in the CPIA from 1999 to 2006; countries without PSR lending did not on average show a major change.

This correlation indicates a combination of two phenomena: (i) Bank support helps improve public sector performance and (ii) a selection process exists whereby countries that are more enthusiastic about PSR (and would improve somewhat anyway) are more likely to get Bank support. Both phenomena are desirable. The statistical analysis cannot tell which phenomenon predominates, and both were present in the case study countries with successful programs.

Whether countries have improved their governance also depends on income level and where they start. Countries in all categories of initial governance and IBRD/IDA were more likely to improve governance if they had a PSR project. Counties with lower initial ratings, say below 3.0, were more likely to improve than those with higher ratings. This is probably because movement in the higher ratings requires more serious changes to the way of doing business, as noted in box 4.1.

A number of countries improved even without Bank lending for PSR, especially those that started at low governance levels. Many countries had as-

sistance from other external sources, even when the Bank was not involved. And some just did it on their own.[3] The Bank's support for PSR is not indispensable, even though it usually does seem to be helpful. Table 4.1 indicates that when there was not lending, IDFs and AAA from the Bank were not consistently correlated with improved public sector performance.

Three-quarters of countries that received PSR lending over 1999–2006 saw an improvement in their governance CPIA measure.

IBRD countries with PSR projects improved more frequently than IDA countries, especially for those with mid-range initial governance ratings. In some cases, such as Cambodia and Honduras civil service, this was because project design was less well adapted to country circumstance for the IDA borrower. A higher degree of self-selection by IBRD borrowers that had PSR lending programs probably also contributed to the difference. Among countries with initially low governance (CPIA lower than 3.0), however, for reasons that are not clear, the rate of improvement for borrowers was higher for the IDA countries than the IBRD countries.

Countries with lower initial ratings were more likely to improve than those with higher ratings.

The Bank—with a variety of tools, international knowledge, and analytic capacity—has a comparative advantage for diagnosis in the technical aspects of the four PSR themes. Discussions with the government counterparts and other donors in the countries visited confirm this perception but also indicate that the extent to which this advantage is used varies across themes and across country types.

In some countries (typically IBRD countries), the government has the financial freedom and in-house technical capacity to decide whether, when, and for what it will borrow for a PSR project. Then the strategy tends to be custom made ("selective") to the country circumstances. But in countries getting major budget support (typically IDA/PRSC), the Bank and donors more often insist on a full array of public sector reforms,

IBRD countries improved more frequently than IDA countries when they had PSR loans.

Table 4.1: Percent of Countries with Improved CPIA Governance Scores by PSR Theme and IDA/IBRD Classification

	IBRD		IDA or blend		Total		Major improvement
	Percent	Number	Percent	Number	Percent	Number	(>0.5) (%)
Any PSR lending	81	31	69	62	73	93	24
With >=2 PSR IL	64	11	73	30	71	41	22
With >=4 PSR AL	25	4	83	12	69	16	6
With IDF(s)	84	19	67	45	72	64	25
Without IDF	75	12	76	17	76	29	21
No PSR lending	54	26	38	16	48	42	5
With IDF(s)	44	9	50	6	47	15	7
With AAA (only)	56	16	31	13	45	29	7

Source: WB CPIA scores and IEG staff calculations.

Note: Entries show the percent and number of countries that show an improvement in the average of CPIA 13–16 between the years 1999 and 2006 (or closest year available). Columns classify countries by their 1999 IBRD/IDA classification. Rows provide this figure for subsets of countries based on the number and type of investment loans (IL) approved or active fiscal 1999–2006 and DPLs (AL) approved in fiscal 1999–2006. AAA = analytical and advisory activities; IBRD = International Bank for Reconstruction and Development; IDA = International Development Association; IDF = institutional development funds; PSR = public sector reform.

and staff often lack the time and resources to design a fully tailored product. So the result is likely to be one size fits all, off the shelf.

The relatively favorable experience with PSR in the IBRD (middle-income) countries, where the leverage of lending rarely motivates reform, shows that the Bank can motivate reforms on the basis of its high-quality expertise and advice. (See also the discussion on project ratings.) Especially in an area such as PSR, where long-term commitment is essential—one-off decisions and turnkey operations will never suffice—success has come if and only when the experts work over time with government counterparts to design and implement a project that fits local circumstances.

Regional differences in results

Just as the incidence of lending varied across Regions, so did the correlation of PSR lending with changes governance scores (see table 4.2). Europe and Central Asia has the highest rate of improvement for countries getting PSR lending— 90 percent—but the rate of improvement for nonborrowers is almost as high. Clearly something else is going on: European Union accession.

Almost all the countries in Europe and Central Asia not borrowing for PSR in 1999–2006 were among the first from the East to join the European Union and had done a lot of reforms with Bank support before 1999.

Latin America and the Caribbean had the second highest rate of improvement for PSR borrowers and a high differential with nonborrowers. In this Region, the improvement rate for IDA was above IBRD (both categories having significant numbers of countries). Africa and East Asia both had 70 percent improvement rates for borrowers, with Africa having the larger differential from the nonborrowers. The Middle East and North Africa and South Asia have the lowest percentages of improvement in governance CPIA scores for PSR borrowers.

IEG Project Ratings

Another source of evidence on these projects is the ratings provided by IEG. Of the 238 PSR projects that closed during calendar years 1999 through 2006, three-quarters of PSR projects with IEG ratings received an overall outcome rating of at least

Table 4.2: Percent of Countries with Improved Governance CPIA Scores by Region, 1999–2006

Region	With Bank PSR lending		Without Bank PSR lending	
	Percent	Number	Percent	Number
Sub-Saharan Africa	70	30	47	15
East Asia and Pacific	70	10	56	9
Europe and Central Asia	90	20	86	7
Latin America and the Caribbean	75	20	25	8
Middle East and North Africa	57	7	0	2
South Asia	50	6	0	1
Total	73	93	48	42

Source: World Bank CPIA scores and IEG staff calculations.

Note: Entries show the percent and number of countries with an improvement in the average of CPIA 13–16 between 1999 and 2006 (or closest year available). Columns classify countries by their 1999 IBRD/IDA classification. Rows provide this figure for subsets of countries based on the number and type of investment loans approved or active fiscal 1999–2006 and development policy loans approved in fiscal 1999–2006.

"moderately satisfactory" and almost half received a rating of "satisfactory" or "highly satisfactory" (table 4.3).[4] Project design (quality-at-entry) and supervision received usually received more favorable ratings on overall outcome, which suggests that the main source of difficulty is with the countries' performance. Another factor, however, is that project objectives (against which outcomes are judged) are sometimes overly ambitious, which pulls down the outcome ratings. More modest objectives with the same substantive projects would have led to higher ratings.

PSR projects to IBRD countries received a larger share of "satisfactory" outcome ratings ("moderately satisfactory," "satisfactory," and "highly satisfactory") than IDA and blend countries. Differences between development policy and investment lending projects were mixed but were generally small. Projects in the Europe and Central Asia Region

Table 4.3: Summary of IEG Project Ratings for Closed PSR Projects, 1999–2006

	All PSR projects	Lending instrument		Lending classification			Region					
		Invest-ment	Adjust-ment	IBRD	Blend	IDA	Sub-Saharan Africa	East Asia and Pacific	Europe and Central Asia	Latin America and the Caribbean	Middle East and North Africa	South Asia
Overall outcome rating												
Percent S or HS	43	37	45	55	43	35	37	22	67	41	20	41
Percent MS, S, or HS	74	67	78	81	75	69	68	61	92	70	60	86
Overall Bank performance rating												
Percent S or HS	79	66	85	89	78	73	68	78	92	84	70	86
Percent MS, S, or HS	80	67	86	91	78	74	69	78	92	88	70	86

Source: IEG Project ratings database and IEG staff calculations.

Note: Table includes projects with significant PSR components that closed between January 1, 1999, and December 31, 2006, and have received IEG project ratings (238 projects). Rows indicate when cells provide the percent of projects with marginally satisfactory (MS), satisfactory (S), or highly satisfactory (HS) ratings.

performed the best on average, with South Asia and Latin America and the Caribbean Region also doing better than the others.

Projects implemented in countries with higher CPIA governance scores[5] received higher project ratings. For example, 67 percent of countries with a 1999 CPIA score above 4.0 received at least a "satisfactory" IEG outcome rating, whereas only 54 percent of projects implemented in countries with a 1999 CPIA score of 2.0–2.5 received this rating in the same period. In particular, projects in countries with high governance scores scored exceptionally high in the borrower preparation, implementation, and compliance ratings.

In a sense, this result is not surprising, but it raises the question of why PSR projects are not better designed and implemented in the countries that need reform most urgently—according to the Bank's own ratings. From the case study evidence, it seems that expectations are often unrealistic and the projects sometimes fail to take care of basic matters first, especially in countries where the basics are most often missing. It is also possible that the government commitment is less predictable in the countries with weak governance, making it more likely that outcomes would fall below the satisfactory range even if the expected outcomes (ex ante objectives) were unbiased on average.

Projects implemented in countries with higher CPIA governance scores generally received higher project ratings.

The success rates for PSR projects—measured by IEG ratings—was higher for IBRD loans than for IDA credits. The reasons for this are not evident in the statistics, but the country cases suggest two possible explanations. First, the design of reforms is sometimes based on models for developed countries, which are too complex for still-developing countries. And the gap is greater for the IDA countries, which tend to have institutions that are further from those of developed countries for which the models are developed.

Second, the expectations and objectives in heavy budget-support projects tend to be more ambitious and global, reflecting the donors' list of things that need fixing rather than the government's list of things it is ready to do. So the reason for the lower success rate in IDA countries may have been that IBRD borrowers had a stronger say in selecting project components, including conditions.

Ratings of IDF grants, most of them for PFM, have improved overall (IEG 2007). For grants approved between fiscal 2002 and 2005, relevance was rated satisfactory in 99 percent, outcome in 79 percent, sustainability in 72 percent, Bank performance in 90 percent, and client performance in 77 percent. Relevance, sustainability, and Bank performance showed the greatest improvement since 2001. Procurement grants had the lowest performance, with less than 70 percent of the grants rated as satisfactory. Financial management grants (including auditing) performed at levels similar to the whole group; however, differences across Regions were substantial. Financial management grants included several best-practice cases, as in Thailand and Turkey.

Interviews in some country visits indicated that the government counterparts do not take IDFs as seriously as loans. Quality of supervision also remains a problem in IDF implementation. Supervision quality has depended on the availability of the task team leader and was usually better with a team leader based in the field. Continuity is also important: the few grants for which team leaders were changed more than once had lower ratings for quality of supervision (IEG 2007).

Reasons for Country Differences

Some of the outcome differentials result from thematic factors discussed in the next chapter, but others are more cross cutting. In all four thematic areas of PSR, the Bank concentrates on the formal rules and regulations, and where divergence from actual practices is recognized, the most common strategy is to fix the formal rules in ways that encourage greater compliance and/or reduce opportunities for corruption. Such a tactic makes sense for an institution like the Bank, which works mainly with the executive branch of government. However, it is often done without much knowledge of what created the problem in the first place and without a clear understanding of the informal processes that typically determine the outcomes.

Some country cases show that the Bank's understanding has improved regarding the difference between formal managerial processes and the practices that actually take place, driven by political economy factors. Guatemala, Bolivia, Honduras, and India are examples of relatively good practice. The Bank has to some extent taken the differences between formal process rules and administrative practices into account in designing and carrying out its support for PFM and taxes. Civil service and corruption have proven more difficult and less successful.

World Bank guidelines (World Bank 2001) recommended substantial participation by clients in PFM data gathering and analysis to facilitate ownership by clients of the results of the analysis. Since 2001, the country cases have shown a mixed record of the Bank's PERs and other PFM AAA being more responsive to demand from borrower countries, including the private sector and civil society as well as government. Bank assistance has also been more active in helping to shape the demand. Good examples were noted in Bangladesh, Tanzania, Uganda, and Vietnam. In some places, such as Bulgaria, the Russian Federation, and Ghana (until recently), the Bank had a productive interaction with the government but not with civil society.

Reasons for shortcomings include lack of incentives for Bank staff to disseminate AAA findings, Bank focus on supply-side rather than demand-side interventions, and concern among Bank staff that civil society awareness raising constitutes political lobbying, which is forbidden by the Bank's charter. This is part of a broader issue: under matrix management—according to interviews with staff—the Bank has gotten better at building cutting-edge skills, but not at integrating knowledge in support of operations at the country level.

The Bank's understanding of political economy is improving, but much of it is still at a general level,

without connection to details of the PSR agenda. Increasingly, there is agreement that a governance assessment is needed before a country proceeds to specific public sector reforms. Addressing corruption, for instance, requires understanding the nature of governance in the particular country. For this, the Bank has done much less. Through fiscal 2006 there were more than 20 IGRs, on a variety of topics, but only 5 of them gave serious attention to the political economy of the public sector as a whole. It is this sector that drives corruption and other aspects of the PSR agenda being evaluated here.

The Bank has improved its responsiveness to borrowers, the Bank's matrix management has caused some problems.

Only in a few cases (for example, Bangladesh, Bolivia, and Peru) have such analyses fed into the PSR pillar of a CAS. Some argue that this is not the comparative advantage of the Bank, given its constitutional requirement to stay out of internal politics and its dependence on the permission of governments to do its work. But the official position of the World Bank Group, reflected in presidential statements and backed by much evidence, is that fundamental improvements in PSM require political commitment and are important for growth and poverty reduction.

The Bank has done some work and could do more to understand the political foundations of governance in its partner countries. Collaborative work, especially involving local researchers, is useful in this area, and the Bank could and occasionally does take the lead in sponsoring such research. Some of this was done informally (India, Mexico, and Tanzania), but usually it is done without as much attention as to items in the regular work program.[6] Internal budget constraints have hindered such work in many smaller countries, where PREM staff do not have much time or money left after doing the standard macroeconomic work. As the IMF already covers that base, the Bank might consider a public sector/political economist, rather than a macroeconomist, as the core of its team in some countries.

The Bank has been improving its understanding of political economy in its partner countries but needs to do more, particularly engaging local research.

Chapter 5

Evaluation Essentials

- Performance measures usually improved for financial management and tax administration, where Bank lending supported such reforms.
- Measures for CSA systems—essential for sustaining other reform areas—did not improve on average. So improving the strategic framework and indicators needs high priority.
- Bank-supported programs for core PSR have rarely succeeded in reducing overall corruption, but have had some success in improving transparency.
- The thematic differences in outcomes result in part from financial management and tax administration being less politically and culturally sensitive than issues surrounding public employment and corruption.
- Bank practices also seem to have contributed to the differences in outcome.

Government building in Putrajaya, Malaysia. Photo © gferro.com.

Public Sector
Reform Outcomes
and Performance
by Thematic Area

In addition to the differences in success across country groups, there are also important differences across thematic areas of PSR. This chapter lays out those differences and looks at country experiences for explanations.

Overview of Thematic Differences

The statistical evidence follows from the same methods as in chapter 4—looking at the percentage of countries in which the CPIA improved. The difference is that in this chapter the ratings for the individual thematic areas are used. Table 5.1 shows that for all countries (with CPIA information), improvement was most likely—60–70 percent likely—in PFM (CPIA 13) and revenue administration (CPIA 14)[1] for countries getting projects in those areas. Quality of public administration (CPIA 15), which we take as civil service reform, had the lowest success rate, with fewer than 45 percent of borrowers in this area showing improvement.

For transparency and anticorruption, the success rate was just over half for countries that had PSR lending in any of the thematic areas. Similar results obtain when considering only projects with explicit (direct) transparency and anticorruption components. It seemed more appropriate to consider PSR lending in any theme, because all themes aim to improve transparency and reduce corruption as at least collateral objectives.

Outcomes for IDA and IBRD countries were similar for PFM and civil service. For tax administration reform, the IDA countries did a little better than IBRD countries. This shows the importance of attention to tax collection even in places where the tax bases look meager. For transparency and anticorruption, however, the success rate for IBRD was considerably higher (almost equal to that with PFM), and the success rate was much lower for ACT among IDA borrowers. The question for the rest of this chapter is why we see these patterns.

Public financial management

What was the support for PFM trying to achieve? The framework for analyzing and improving PFM came mostly from upper-income countries. Among the PFM reforms pursued by Organisation for Economic Co-operation and Development (OECD) countries over the past 25 years, eight broad components are noteworthy (OECD 1995; Brumby 1999; Pollitt and Bouchaert 2004; Rubin and Kelly 2005):

- Achieving budget savings through more robust central controls or by

Eight components of financial management are notable in the reforms pursued by OECD countries.

Table 5.1: Changes in Selected CPIA Scores by PSR Theme, Initial Governance Score, and IDA/IBRD Classification

	IBRD		IDA or blend		Total		Major improvement (>0.5)	
	Percent	Number of countries	Percent	Number of countries	Percent	Number of countries	Percent	Number of countries
CPIA (13)—Quality of budget and financial management								
Any PSR PFM lending	64	28	61	59	62	87	28	87
No PSR PFM lending	21	29	32	19	25	48	10	48
CPIA (15)—Quality of public administration								
Any PSR CSA lending	44	18	42	53	42	71	10	71
No PSR CSA lending	41	39	20	25	33	64	16	64
CPIA (14) —Efficiency of revenue mobilization								
Any PSR TAX lending	67	18	73	26	70	44	32	44
No PSR TAX lending	46	39	56	52	52	91	21	91
CPIA (16) —Corruption, transparency and accountability								
Any PSR lending	61	31	48	62	53	93	26	93
No PSR lending	38	26	44	16	40	42	7	42

Source: World Bank CPIA scores and IEG staff calculations.

Note: Entries show the percent and number of countries that show an improvement in the respective CPIA score between the years 1999 and 2006 (or closest year available). Columns classify countries by their 1999 IBRD/IDA classification. Rows provide this figure for subsets of countries based on the number and type of investment loans approved or active fiscal 1999–2006 and development policy loans approved fiscal 1999–2006. CPIA = Country Policy and Institutional Assessment; IBRD = International Bank for Reconstruction and Development; IDA = International Development Association; PFM = public finance management; PSR = public sector reform; TAX = tax administration.

providing greater flexibility to managers and organizations in reallocating funds within budget line items to reflect changing conditions and priorities

- Restructuring budgets to include expenditures for all government activities, global budgetary targets, hard budget constraints, and program allocations to facilitate results monitoring and evaluation
- A multiyear budget linked to a realistic fiscal policy and revenue estimates
- Regular use of performance information in monitoring against targets to facilitate accountability and manage performance
- Shifting from cost accounting[2] toward accrual accounting[3]
- Shifting from compliance auditing[4] toward performance auditing[5]

- Computerized information systems providing timely financial and related information to all parties in the budget process
- Greater use of devolved budget management and market-based mechanisms, such as user and capital charges, market testing, outsourcing, and performance agreements.

Most of the countries receiving PFM support are doing better in that area, as noted earlier, which is consistent with the more detailed results of Levy and Kpundeh (2004) for a sample of African countries. In examining why this happened and what the limits to success are, the following questions are relevant:

- Have PFM reforms first rolled out in developed countries been transferred and adapted appropriately to developing country settings?

- Did the Bank understand the differences between formal, managerial processes and the practices that actually take place, and did it take the differences into account in designing and carrying out its support?
- Has the bank stressed "getting the basics right" before supporting more complex financial management reforms?
- Has PFM in sector ministries been a better entry point than PFM in core ministries, or vice versa? Have PFM projects/components been usefully piloted in sector ministries before wider rollouts have taken place? Has PFM in subnational jurisdictions been a useful entry point?
- Has the Bank's PFM approach resulted in improved public sector performance? Were the benefits achieved greater than the costs incurred? In what technical areas and country contexts has the Bank been effective/ineffective and why?

The Bank's *Public Expenditure Management Handbook* (World Bank 1998b) stresses the importance of getting the basics right first: Control inputs before seeking to control outputs, account for cash before moving to accrual accounting, operate a reliable budget for inputs before moving to budgeting for results, make a comprehensive budget and reliable accounting system before trying an integrated financial management system, get a proper budgeting and accounting function before strengthening the auditing function, and do reliable financial auditing before trying performance auditing (Schick 1998; Shand 2001).

Evidence from case studies shows favorable results where the Bank followed this advice. In countries such as Bulgaria, which is working to meet the standards for admission to the European Union, improving basic PFM has been an important part of the agenda. In Guatemala, the Integrated Financial Management System program supported basic public finance building blocks (improved budgeting, accounting, frameworks, and cash management) and well-sequenced capacity building. Progress has taken place even in weak capacity countries just emerging from conflict, such as Sierra Leone, which has improved

transparency, procurement, accountability in budget execution, and audits (internal and external).

In some other places, however, such as Ghana, Indonesia, and initially Honduras, the Bank supported the installation of systems that turned out to be overly complex. Guyana's PFM program in the 1990s was also overly complex, leading to problems at various stages of procurement and implementation. When Bank support for PFM restarted there after 2000, it concentrated more on the basics first.

Ambitious PFM reforms in the Republic of Yemen could have used a more incremental approach, starting with core treasury systems and a general ledger and then building broader capacity and commitment for more extensive reforms. An advanced financial management information system supported by the Bank, although showing initial results, may be difficult to sustain in a low-capacity environment.

Similarly, financial management information technology systems have been successfully adopted in some cases when there are sufficient commitment, capacity, and resources as part of a broad and appropriately phased reform program, with significant efficiency gains if conditions are right. In places with weak capacity, however, such as are found in many Bank borrowers, the principal benefit from information technology may be ensuring more systematic adherence to financial rules by manual systems, which finance staff may rely on more, as the older systems run in parallel to technology-based systems.

The evidence is also mixed on the related question of whether PFM reforms first tried in developed countries have been transferred with appropriate adaptations to local conditions in developing country settings. An early innovation was Bolivia's 1990 Financial Management and Control Law, which sought to increase the efficiency and effectiveness of the public sector by switching from a centralized rule-based system to a more modern, decentralized, results-oriented system. Enacted

The Bank's handbook on public expenditure management stresses the importance of getting the basics right first.

Case studies show favorable results where PFM reforms did address the basics first.

Financial management reforms first tried in developed countries have sometimes—but not always—had appropriate adaptations for application in developing countries.

because of strong pressure from the Bank and other donors, it lacked sufficient incentives for public officials to enforce it. As a result, the required annual operating plans were formally undertaken as a ritual, but were ignored when it came to agency programming and resource allocation (Dove 2002).

Another type of innovation introduced in developed countries and now being promoted by the Bank among borrower countries is a multiyear perspective in fiscal planning, expenditure policy, and budgeting. Despite concerns about achieving transparency in multiyear budgeting and despite challenges evident in developed countries in making effective use of this tool (Oxford Policy Management 2000), MTEFs are central features of the Poverty Reduction Strategy Papers and PRSCs prepared in recent years. Craig and Porter (2003) point out that aside from technical problems of using this tool effectively, its use for upward accountability to central ministries and donors can undermine local political legitimacy and accountability, sideline the role of legislatures, and cut off important sources of local knowledge on what works and what does not in poverty reduction. Many developing countries have followed the example of developed countries in adopting this reform to help achieve greater certainty on future funding from donors.

Although MTEFs have been challenging for many developed countries, Albania, Burkina Faso, South Africa, Tanzania, and Uganda have adopted well-functioning systems, with Bank support. Such an innovation can be especially useful for a borrower in a context of high aid dependency, where the big uncertainty on the revenue side is donor support. Tanzania's MTEF helps coordinate commitment from the donors, which fund more than 40 percent of the budget, and thus helps get enough certainty on the revenue side to plan the budget. Implementation and utilization of the MTEF has been more difficult in Mali and Ghana.

Some countries have adopted well-functioning MTEFs with Bank support, although such frameworks have been challenging for many.

Slovakia has an MTEF, implemented with Bank support, that also includes

program budgeting and a firmer (compared with previous years) ceiling for the current year and indicative ceilings for the next two years. This framework had the benefit of discouraging the past practice of submitting budget requests that are out of line with available resources. Program budgeting is still considered separately from the real budget preparation, however; there is little time devoted to substance; performance indicators focus on outputs rather than outcomes; and program managers are not accountable for results. In addition, budget execution does not take place on a programmatic basis, which reinforces the view that the program budget is not the real budget. Even where MTEFs are proving useful, a less-detailed and more strategic planning exercise might serve the purpose better.

Entry points are important, as noted above; PFM and tax administration are good thematic entry points, and AAA is a good entry instrument—such as PERs, CPARs, CFAAs, and PETS. Within the limits of PFM project activities, the question of entry points also arises. Some countries found it helpful to pilot nascent MTEFs and other reforms in ministries or subnational governments with demonstrated PFM capacity, to draw lessons from the pilot, and then to gradually scale up to other ministries.

Argentina, Cambodia, India (state level), Russia, and Tanzania were good examples. These initiatives were most successful when core ministries—finance and planning—provided the support and space for the sectoral or subnational interventions to succeed. Although entry points were mainly finance ministries or departments in ministries or subnational authorities, the Bank also supported legislative oversight and civil society initiatives in Ghana, for example.

Regarding lending instruments, there has been a shift toward more flexible, long-term lending instruments since 2000. This includes a shift in PFM support from investment to programmatic policy-based loans. The results of this shift are broadly favorable, with strong performance in Ghana, Guatemala, and Tanzania, for example. PFM outcomes tied to HIPC accession and PRSCs proved fruitful in Ghana, Honduras, Tanzania, and Uganda. Yet the delayed treasury system in Indonesia and the modest PFM improvements evident in Uganda point to continuing challenges under the new instruments.

In Mali, investment lending—rather than or in addition to policy-based lending—might have achieved better results. In Guyana, India, Russia, and Tanzania, the continuation of PSR investment lending, in parallel with Policy Reform Loans and often with longer-term instruments, was important to sustain support for reforms.

The Bank has been cautious in considering the use of procurement processes of governments or other donors, usually preferring the processes in the PIUs it sponsors rather than using government systems.[6] This can slow down improvements in government systems and exacerbate the delays in information technology projects, and it still does not ensure that procurement will be corruption free (see table 5.2).

For example, decentralized procurement in Honduras within the ministries and agencies has languished for lack of capacity and because perceptions of corruption make donors reluctant to channel resources through the regular civil service. Instead, a proliferation of PIUs has led to expensive and fragmented procurement managed under a host of balkanized rules and regulations. Procurement delays in Ghana, Guyana, and Indonesia, among other countries, have hampered PFM support, although this seems to be improving. The U.S. Millennium Challenge Corporation recently agreed to use the new information management systems for the management of its program in Honduras. This is a notable achievement, given the strict requirements of the U.S. government.

Investment projects for PFM and tax administration typically put a strong emphasis on technology and sometimes carried the expectation that it would be the main key to results, without adequately recognizing that changes of incentives, behavior, and organizational cultures are more important and more challenging (see box 5.1). Even when the people-management aspects were recognized in the project design, if these more difficult aspects of the projects hit snags, the tech-

The Bank has often used PIUs rather than government procurement systems, but this slows government improvements without ensuring corruption-free procurement.

Table 5.2: Improvement Rates in Public Financial Management (CPIA 13) by IDA/IBRD Classification

	CPIA (13) quality of budget and financial management and PFM PSR lending, 1999–2006							
	IBRD		IDA or blend		Total		Major improvement (>0.5)	
	Percent	Number	Percent	Number	Percent	Number	Percent	Number
Any PSR PFM lending	64	28	61	59	62	87	28	87
With >= 2 PSR PFM IL	29	7	64	22	55	29	28	29
With >= 4 PSR PFM AL	67	3	82	11	79	14	21	14
With PFM IDF	79	14	68	37	71	51	31	51
Without PFM IDF	50	14	50	22	50	36	22	36
No PSR PFM lending	21	29	32	19	25	48	10	48
With PFM IDF	20	10	38	8	28	18	17	18
With any AAA	26	19	31	16	29	35	14	35

Source: World Bank CPIA scores and IEG staff calculations.

Note: Entries show the percent and number of countries that show an improvement in the average of CPIA 13 between the years 1999 and 2006 (or closest year available). Columns classify countries by their 1999 IBRD/IDA classification. Rows provide this figure for subsets of countries based on the number and type of investment loans (IL) approved or active fiscal 1999–2006 and development policy loans (AL) approved in fiscal 1999–2006. AAA = analytical and advisory activities; IBRD = International Bank for Reconstruction and Development; IDA = International Development Association; IDF = institutional development funds; PFM = public financial management; PSR = public sector reform.

Box 5.1: Too Much Attention to the Technical Aspects—Not Enough to the Human Element in Ghana

The Public Financial Management Technical Assistance Project in Ghana had an information management system component that was overly complex, when simple spreadsheets could have done the job. It created "a very big conceptual, technical, and managerial challenge" and left gaps in policies and outputs. It did not link "the poor performance with the mandates, role, organizational structures, overlapping responsibilities, outdates procedures and processes, and skill levels," nor did it flag the issue of availability for training. There were too many components for the PIU and government to effectively coordinate, and the implementation schedule was overambitious. Functional units should have been given responsibility for implementing reforms rather than the PIU, which was recommended in the midterm review but which was not done.

Source: World Bank 2004d.

nology parts of the project often continued to disburse despite the changed conditions that reduced their effectiveness.

In the area of PFM, the Bank's analytic work has progressed furthest. A review of 50 recent development policy operations found that more than half were informed by at least three PFM studies by the Bank and other development partners (Parison 2005). The number of PERs has increased from 17 per year for 1999–2002 to more than 23 annually since then.

Increased attention is now given to institutional aspects. Initially, the focus was almost exclusively on budget formulation—setting aggregates and sectoral allocations—but since 2000 more attention has gone to the execution phase of the budget cycle. PERs are now routinely (although still not always) linked with CFAAs and CPARs, which now include governmentwide assessments and sometimes subnational governments.[7] The PETS has proven to be a powerful addition to the Bank's toolkit for identifying problems with (and corruption in) expenditure and financial management, although the cost and time demands have made PETS impractical for universal application.

CFAAs and CPARs helped increase the focus on PFM issues in subsequent country strategies.

A recent IEG evaluation (IEG 2007) found that 64 percent of CPARs and 71

percent of CFAAs were of satisfactory quality, with steady improvement in quality since the publication of the respective guidelines and with increased donor collaboration. They could have been more effective, however, with improved coordination among the units preparing them and other PFM reports; they could have avoided confusing situations such as clients getting multiple PFM action plans.

Despite these shortcomings, CFAAs and CPARs contributed to a greater focus on PFM in subsequent CASs and to increased PFM lending. CASs in 13 of the 22 countries studied proposed DPLs with PFM prior actions and conditions, and only 4 CASs proposed such lending prior to the completion of the CFAAs/CPARs. Likewise, twice as many CASs since 2000 proposed PFM investment lending as was proposed in countries prior to the completion of CFAAs/CPARs. These instruments have only had a modest overall impact, however, on PFM and procurement arrangements and on the choice of instruments for Bank assistance (IEG 2007, pp. 37, 41–42).

Routine monitoring of public expenditure management has improved greatly since the late 1990s, first with the HIPC tracking process and more recently with the PEFA indicators. The interest in ensuring good management of HPIC resources evolved into interest in ensuring that general budget support, with instruments such as PRSCs, went through efficient, transparent, and socially accountable processes.

This led the Bank, along with other partners and in consultation with many governments, to develop the PEFA indicators.[8] These focus on the PFM process but also include a little on tax administration, civil service, corruption, and reliability of donor funding. There are 28 major indicators of country performance, most with subindicators, plus three indicators of donor practices, such as predictability of direct budget support.

Building on the three budgetary outcomes discussed above, the indicators measure six dimensions: budget credibility, comprehensiveness and transparency, alignment with policy, predictability and control, accounting and reporting, and external scrutiny and audit (see PEFA Secretariat 2005 for a complete listing). They indicate gradations of improvement in PSM, corresponding to a sequence, and provide a range of standards that includes OECD countries, some of which are also rated. PEFA is thus a model for what could be extended to or replicated in other PSR thematic areas.[9]

As of August 2007, 40 countries had completed one or more PEFA assessments.[10] PEFA and other related indicators are useful because they measure actual practice, rather than perception or reputation, and they look at actions that would be the immediate objectives of reform.

An analysis of 15 countries with both HIPC and PEFA ratings looked at 11 indicators where there is close correspondence between the two assessment methods. Over the period 2001–2006, five countries showed improvement in the number of HIPC benchmarks met (with Ghana improving by six benchmarks), six showed a decline, and four remained largely unchanged. Based on raw scores, eight countries improved, four declined, and three were unchanged.

In terms of the different phases of the budget cycle, the greatest improvement was in budget reporting, with less improvement in budget formulation and some deterioration in budget execution. At a more detailed level, more than 90 percent of countries could limit the discrepancies between budget allocations and budget outturns in 2006, compared with less than 50 percent in 2004. Eighty percent of countries met the benchmark on improvements in budget classification in 2006, the same as in 2004. However, there was a decline in the quality of medium-term projections in budget processes and in ability to reflect donor funds in the budget (de Renzio and Dorotinsky 2007).

Some HIPC countries, where the Bank's work on PFM issues has been intense, have more detailed records of progress. Taking the 23 countries participating in HIPC that were monitored first in 2001

and then again in 2003–04 and considering the benchmarks set for 15 PFM elements, the number of countries meeting or exceeding the benchmarks increased for 8 indicators, declined for 6, and stayed the same for 1. Of the three main PFM areas (see appendix A), budget reporting improved the most, with 14 countries improving and 4 worsening.

Routine monitoring of public expenditure management has improved with the use of PEFA indicators, which measure practice rather than perception or reputation.

Within this indicator group is, for example, the indicator 13: "Regular fiscal reports track poverty reducing spending." Here the number of countries meeting the benchmark increased from three to seven. Forty-two percent of benchmarks in the "reporting" area were met in 2004, up from 33 percent in 2001.

In the other two PFM areas of "formulation" and "execution," however, there were modest declines between the two reporting periods in countries meeting the benchmarks (World Bank and IMF 2006).[11] Traditionally, the Bank gave more attention to budget formulation than to budget execution, and traditional financial management looked mainly at Bank projects, not the whole spending cycle. Somewhat more attention now goes to the downstream aspects, but more consistent effort is still needed in that direction.

In summary, the Bank's increased PFM lending and analytical work can be linked with encouraging PFM improvements among borrowers, usefully adapting PFM tools from other jurisdictions, and carrying out effective monitoring with robust assessment tools accepted by major donors. However, progress is uneven, both across countries and across different types of indicators. Bank performance might have achieved greater success with deeper institutional and governance analysis, greater attention to addressing basic systems before moving to advanced PFM tools, and more Bank support and flexibility in working to improve countries' own procurement systems. Conditionality worked better when it focused on PSR outcomes, leaving country governments to pick specific

The Bank's increased PFM lending and analytical work can be linked to encouraging PFM improvements among its borrowers.

measures and the Bank to give technical assistance on request.

CSA reform design

What was the support for CSA reform trying to achieve? This thematic area of reform includes several components:

- *Measures to track the existing staff*—for instance, developing computerized payroll and human resources databases—are usually an important early reform action without much controversy. Pay and employment data are often missing, and these data are essential to diagnosing civil service issues and designing reforms.
- *Measures to contain and reduce the number of staff*—via retrenchment and layoffs, early retirement, and hiring freezes—are usually the most controversial components of CSA reform.
- *Compensation reforms* deal with pay structures and pensions.
- *Human resource management* reforms deal with management of cadres generally and the senior civil service particularly. This includes merit-based recruitment, promotion and discipline, performance management, and appraisal systems.
- *Organizational reforms* deal with issues such as contracting, creating delivery agencies, and process engineering and organizational restructuring. These issues are usually based on functional and program reviews and aim to improve operational efficiency.
- *Demand-side reforms* focus on the users of services, through service standards, e-government, and so forth.
- *Training and capacity building*.

Table 5.3 compares the different CSA reform components in terms of political risk, financial implications, and demands on capacity.

The Bank used to emphasize retrenchment and salary decompression among CSA reforms— an approach that usually failed.

The Bank's involvement in CSA reforms evolved out of the need to address the issue of an affordable wage bill as a significant component of public sector expenditures. As a result, CSA reforms often emphasized (especially in the 1980s and 1990s) retrenchment and salary decompression (increases at the top). But this focus often overlooked indications that these actions were politically unrealistic and also assumed without evidence that these changes would bring about improved public administration. This approach usually failed, because the downsizing either did not take place or was reversed by rehiring, often of the same people. Since then, the Bank has continued to endorse the same formula with similar lack of success in 1999–2006, although in fewer countries, such as Cambodia, Honduras, and the Republic of Yemen.

In the past few years, the Bank has shifted its focus in many countries to human resource management reforms, such as merit-based recruitment and promotion, both as a means to improve performance and as a counter to patronage-based systems. Drawing on project conditionality as a proxy for the Bank's activity in this area, the focus on merit-based measures has grown significantly in the past five years; downsizing is somewhat less prominent (see figure 5.1).

In the 19 case studies, the reforms most frequently supported with Bank programs since 1999 include payroll and human resources databases, redeployment/layoff provisions, pay reforms, merit recruitment and promotion, and training/capacity-building programs. The Bank has continued to advocate downsizing and pay reforms, but merit-related reforms have risen in importance since 2000 (see also Stevens and Teggemann 2004.)

Database reforms and training have also been common elements of many reform packages, in part because of their less controversial nature as well as their direct linkage to other reform areas, particularly PFM. An important step in many countries has been to get the human resource database and the payroll (usually at the ministries of finance) consistent with each other.

For administrative reforms, the bulk of activity has centered on functional reviews, at times to support downsizing efforts but also as a means to improve operational efficiencies. In Russia, some redun-

Table 5.3: Civil Service and Administrative Reform: Types and Challenges

Component	Political risk	Financial cost	Demanding of capacity	Successfully implemented reforms	Little or no progress
Pay and employment data	Minimal	Modest	Yes—but capacity building is part of project	Rep. of Yemen, Guyana	Honduras, Uganda
Downsizing	High	Significant one-time costs for retrenchment	Yes, to do it right (targeted)	Russia, Tanzania, India	Bulgaria, Guyana, Uganda, Ethiopia, Rep. of Yemen, Cambodia, Sri Lanka
Compensation reforms	Yes, in egalitarian cultures, where lower ranks are politicized or where unions are strong	Yes	Yes	Bulgaria, Albania	Guyana, Indonesia, Rep. of Yemen Pakistan
Human resource management reforms	Yes, especially in patgronage-based systems	Moderate	Yes	Bulgaria, Bolivia (pilots), Albania	Ghana
Organizational reforms	Moderate	Modest	Yes	Russia, India, Tanzania	Ghana
Demand-side reforms	Moderate	Modest	Yes	Tanzania, Uganda, India	
Training	No	Modest	No	Ethiopia, Russia, Rep. of Yemen	Bolivia

Source: IEG country case studies.

dant or duplicative functions were eliminated; in Ghana, some minor process improvements have been reported. However, in other case studies, these reviews generally did not lead to real process changes. There has been some reform effort focused on restructuring, including agency automation, such as in Tanzania. On demand-side reforms, citizen charters, standards of service, or other mechanisms like client service units and surveys have been introduced in some countries (Ghana, India, Russia, Tanzania, and Uganda), with favorable results beginning to show in some places.

Outcomes. Despite the continued efforts and some modification of the approach, civil service reform has been relatively unsuccessful, as is apparent from table 5.3. A similar table using a non-Bank indicator (the public administration rating of the ICRG) also gave an unsatisfactory result. Also, countries getting more Bank loans (development policy or investment) for CSA reform did not do better on average than those getting only one. The question is, why? And why were there successes in some cases?

The case studies show that reform in the area of CSA has been extremely challenging, even in a relatively supportive environment. The cases highlighted a number of country-specific reasons why

In the past five years, merit-based measures for civil service reform have increased.

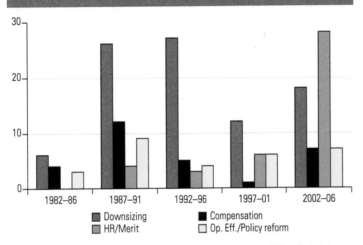

Figure 5.1: Number of CSA Projects with Various Subcategories of Conditions

Legend:
- Downsizing
- HR/Merit
- Compensation
- Op. Eff./Policy reform

Source: Adjustment Lending Conditionality and Implementation Database and IEG staff calculations.

Note: CSA = civil service and administrative; HR = human resources.

ing. In addition, the strength of trade unions in the public sector can subvert downsizing, pay, and merit-based reforms in an otherwise supportive political regime. Concerted government effort partly overcame this in Burkina Faso and Guatemala, but not in Honduras.

Despite these political, cultural, and institutional challenges, the cases give some examples of successful CSA reforms. Six factors seem to have contributed to these successes—and in their absence, likely contributed to reform failures: analytic diagnosis and advice, pragmatic opportunism in selecting reforms to support, realistic external expectations, appropriate packages of lending instruments, tangible indicators of success, and effective donor coordination.

Strong and coherent technical and contextual analysis. For CSA issues, the Bank's analytical tools are relatively underdeveloped and underused. There is no standard Bank diagnostic instrument or report for the analysis of the civil service. The absence of a standard analytical tool is partly a consequence of the lack of international consensus around the "right" civil service model for developing countries, or indeed for developed countries. Debate continues about the objective of CSA reform—whether it is affordability, performance, or accountability—and the sequencing and fit with political realities.

The Bank has rarely analyzed the political considerations that make civil service reform so difficult; the IGRs in Bolivia and Bangladesh are notable exceptions. As a result, many of the case studies attribute part of the failure to make headway in CSA to the narrow scope of the Bank's analytical work.

The diagnostic work done by the Bank on administrative and civil service reform is typically relegated to one chapter of a broader piece of analysis, most often a financial report of some type. In reviewing the country studies, for example, of 69 ESW reports that had some discussion of CSA, only 5 were freestanding analyses of civil service issues; 39 were PERs or other financial reports; 6 were CEMs; and 19 were parts of other broader

implementation of these reforms—particularly downsizing, pay decompression, and merit-based reforms—failed.

Civil service reforms, despite modifications in approach, have remained a relatively difficult and often unsuccessful area of the Bank's assistance.

First and most common, there can be a lack of political commitment to reform or a discontinuity over the implementation period. In some countries, the government may adopt reform strategies and even pass new legislation. But then as implementation starts up, momentum slows, delays occur, and projects can completely stall, such as in Ghana, Argentina, and the Republic of Yemen. This issue of political commitment can affect even the most uncontroversial measures, such as introduction of new data systems, by reallocating resources or simply delaying projects because of staff turnover.

Changes in political leadership can also result in decisions to terminate, reverse, or dilute more controversial reforms such as downsizing. In a number of countries, such as Bangladesh, Ethiopia, and the Republic of Yemen, the persistence of patronage systems and politicization of the bureaucracy undermined implementation in the review period, particularly those reforms that affect pay, recruitment, promotion, and downsiz-

The Bank's analytical tools for analyzing CSA issues are underdeveloped and underused.

papers. Although the number has grown—25 reports during the 1990s, increasing to 44 in the past 7 years—the bias toward using financial reporting vehicles remains strong. As a consequence, the CSA analyses tend to focus on affordability issues rather than on performance or accountability.[12] This is not to deny the importance of affordability, but rather to note that it has not usually proven successful as an entry point for dialogue on civil service reform.

Effective analysis of CSA issues is made more difficult by the scarcity of standardized data, such as numbers of staff by grade and occupation group, as well as data on the wage bill. Nor do standard measures of performance or indicators of reform implementation exist.

Recently, however, there has been some process in this area. For instance, the CPIA question on quality of public administration has four subcomponents: policy coordination and responsiveness, service delivery and operational efficiency, merit and ethics, and pay adequacy and management of the wage bill. WBI governance indicators also measure bureaucracy quality. Although there is no civil service equivalent to PEFA, there have been a few diagnostic pilots in the Europe and Central Asia Region (Albania and the former Yugoslav Republic of Macedonia, for instance) and in some Indian states—measuring rates of turnover, shares of personnel recruited through competitive exams, and so on—but these have not been widely applied in other countries.

Often even basic data are lacking, and initial reforms may involve personnel inventory and information systems. This is sometimes a good opportunity for an entry point to the civil service reform agenda. However, the Bank has not (with other stakeholders) developed or promoted an adequate framework and tools to incorporate CSA issues into the standard diagnostics.

Russia is an example of a country for which the Bank provided good quality analysis and advice on CSA reforms that was well received and valued by the client and that helped support the client's reform agenda. Bolivia and Honduras are

other examples where contextual analysis was carried out to good effect. Understanding labor market conditions has been an important part of successful contextual analyses. Unfortunately, the more common experience has been the opposite—the absence of good diagnosis and analysis can lead to inappropriate reforms or failure to convince governments to take action. This issue was highlighted in a number of case study countries, including Ethiopia, Ghana, Guyana, and Indonesia.

Analytics tend to focus on civil service reform affordability issues rather than on performance.

Taking a pragmatic and opportunistic approach to CSA reforms where the institutional environment is challenging. Ingrained systems of patronage political appointments are often at the root of problems with the civil service, which successful diagnosis has understood. But the Bank's traditional tools, especially lending conditions, are ill suited to addressing this fundamental challenge.

Some positive results are being achieved where the design of reform measures is more pragmatic; the reforms try to shift existing practice rather than advocate all-or-nothing change. Russia, for example, has started to require that new hires meet certain minimum qualifications even if the final selection is politicized, to keep track of absentees, and to make it easier to fire them. In Cambodia, selective, enhanced pay schemes have been used; at first the Bank and IMF staff were unsupportive, concerned that a two-tier salary system would cause friction. But ultimately it was recognized that an informal two-tier system was already in place because of ad hoc donor arrangements and that this program would encourage consistency and a better targeting of resources. Implementation of reforms through pilots—as in Russia—when a more comprehensive approach would likely fail can also be more effective in riskier environments.

Realistic expectations by the donor community. It is now well acknowledged that CSA reforms take time to implement and to show tangible results. Tanzania provides a good example of a reform process where the Bank and other donors have let the government take the lead in terms of pace and direction and have shown patience for building capacity. In this case, the Bank has used a longer-term and more flexible lending instrument (such as an adaptable program loan) and has pooled funds with other donors to respond to this reality.

Other cases, however, show that Bank and other donors can have expectations that are too short term, which inevitably sets the reforms up for failure. The Republic of Yemen offers an example of this. It is also true that unrealistic expectations can be created by the political leadership within the country (such as Ghana), where broad and ambitious strategies are at times promoted and approved, but implementation stalls as vested interests coalesce.

Case studies show that technical assistance funded with investment loans has been particularly important in encouraging civil service reform.

Appropriate package of lending instruments. The case studies show that technical assistance funded with investment loans has been a particularly important tool for encouraging civil service reform, especially in poorer countries where capacity levels are usually very low. In some of the cases, such as Cambodia, Honduras, and Tanzania, the combination of policy-based lending supported by technical assistance was a positive feature, particularly in countries with low capacity for implementation.

In other cases, where only development policy lending supported civil service reform, the lack of supporting technical assistance was a hindrance to progress. Learning from such experiences sometimes led to the revival of investment lending to support civil service reforms. In Uganda, the government did not initially allocate enough budget resources to the CSA reforms; now bilateral funding supports them.

Linking CSA reforms to PFM reforms may help overcome the perceived lack of tangible benefit to CSA reform.

Tangible indicators of success. Unlike tax reform, where leaders see obvious benefits, the political leadership cannot easily identify tangible benefits of CSA reform. Linking CSA reforms to more concrete PFM reforms where possible is one way to address this. Most con-

ducive to this effort is the development of payroll and human resources databases, as well as training and capacity building in support of PFM.

Another strategy is to develop measurable indicators of results. The Albania case study shows some progress in this area, with the Bank supporting the development of a number of civil service–related measures, such as the percentage of recruitment done by merit, which the government is now tracking on a regular basis. These are not final outcome measures, but they provide a more transparent method of demonstrating progress in implementation.

A few other countries are tracking similar measures, such as FYR Macedonia and some Indian states, but there is no standard set of indicators or wide adoption that is similar to the PEFA indicators. Further effort in this area is certainly worth pursuing.

The case study of Russia offers additional insights. Its reform agenda began with economic reforms and then moved to fiscal reforms. Russia has more recently reached the stage where poor capacity is holding back other reforms, and with this realization at the political level, there is now a growing acceptance of the need for civil service reform. Not only has this case shown the importance of building demand for CSA reform through identifying tangible benefits, but it also shows that it is possible to proceed with some elements of reform in the absence of or in advance of comprehensive action.

Effective donor coordination. In some countries, reform strategies have become joint efforts with the donor community, with positive effects. Tanzania, Bulgaria, and Guyana provide good examples, as does Ghana with its joint CAS process. In some cases, the Bank has shown itself to be an effective facilitator, and results have generally been more positive than when it has tried to drive reforms (such as downsizing) in the absence of political commitment. Interestingly, Tanzania's reform agenda suffered in the early years because an uncoordinated approach by donors resulted in conflicting advice and multiple agendas. This situation changed when the government successfully demanded better coordination among donors.

These various Bank strategies to support CSA reforms in the case study countries are consistent with and reflect a number of the recommendations from the 1999 IEG evaluation. For instance, that report emphasized the need to preface reform design with institutional assessments of administrative systems and analyses of labor market trends in addition to budget scenarios. However, this type of analysis is still the exception rather than the norm.

Another recommendation proposed that the Bank engage in a more participatory approach to reform design and implementation. This is now happening, for example, in Tanzania. The Bank has also made progress on the report's recommendation to coordinate better with other donors and focus its input where it has a comparative advantage. In Bulgaria, for example, the Bank provided a roadmap for reform, but other donors provided the technical assistance for specific reforms. The development of standardized performance measures, as is being tried in Albania, was a recommendation from the 1999 report.

Tax administration

What was the support for tax administration trying to achieve, and why did it usually succeed? Tax administration reforms aim—or at least should aim—primarily to increase voluntary compliance. Other important objectives include raising more revenue, reducing evasion, and making the pattern of tax collection and incentives correspond to those intended in the legislation. This evaluation does not discuss tax policy (legislation), although tax administration *is* tax policy in the sense that what actually gets implemented is what matters (Bird and Casanegra de Jantscher 1992). Legislated tax policy also matters for administration, of course, with clarity and the absence of exemptions in the law facilitating collection, compliance, and enforcement.

For tax administration reform, the typical entry point for the Bank's policy dialogue has been the government's need for additional revenue. Other objectives include preparation for accession to the European Union (Bulgaria), adapting tax administration to a free market economy (Russia and other Eastern European countries), and increasing transparency and efficiency to improve the image of tax administration with voters and the business sector.

There have been positive effects where tax reform strategies have become joint efforts with the donor community.

Over the past decades there have been several trends in tax administration reform:

- Reorganization of tax departments along functional lines
- Establishing a comprehensive system of taxpayer identification numbers
- Computerization
- Granting autonomy to tax departments
- Establishment of large taxpayer units.

All these measures helped improve the effectiveness of tax administration, but none was a magic bullet. A judicious combination of these measures with others, such as simplification of procedures, appropriate collection systems, effective audit and appeal mechanisms, adequate human resource policies, and well-designed taxpayer information and service systems, are all necessary to increase the effectiveness of tax administration and reduce opportunities for corruption. Although there is not a unique ideal administrative model that fits all revenue agencies, there is a widely recognized set of administrative strategies that allows experts to usually agree on the main set of reforms needed in a country. Some of these are captured in the PEFA indicators, three of which deal with tax administration, each with three subdimensions.

To develop an appropriate reform strategy, success has depended on starting with a good diagnostic of the problems of the existing tax administration. With respect to both diagnosis and strategy design, it is advisable to profit from work done previously by other donors—for example, the IMF in Albania, Bulgaria, and Tanzania—and complement it with Bank work. A pilot approach to tax administration

The Bank's entry point for tax administration reform has typically been the need to increase revenues.

reform has proven successful in many cases. In some countries, implementation of the value-added tax has been used as a pilot for introducing modern systems of taxpayer identification, tax collection, and so on (for example, Albania). In other countries, the establishment of large taxpayer units has served the same purpose (for example, in Bulgaria and Russia).

Outcomes. Among the 27 countries with tax administration investment projects approved or still active in 1999–2006, more than three-fourths showed improved CPIAs (1999–2006) for revenue mobilization; seven had major improvements. In contrast, among countries with tax administration conditions in DPLs but no investment/technical assistance loans, only a bare majority showed improvement—not much better than in countries with no tax administration lending. Doing a complete reform of tax administration takes some time—most of the Bank's tax administration investment projects lasted five to seven years, and more than 80 percent had to be extended to achieve the desired results. Patience has paid off.

Most of the Bank's tax administration investment projects have been extended, but they have usually paid off. Working with other donors has been important in most of the cases studied. The IMF often helps with the diagnosis and strategy; others, such as DFID and the European Union often help with cofinancing. Still, the role of Bank expertise is important; even when the IMF is providing a lot of technical advice, having the Bank help design and manage the actual project has been essential, according to interviews with country counterparts. And the IMF is not always available; in those cases, the in-house expertise and consultant roster of the Bank become even more important.

On diagnosis and general strategy for tax administration (and treasury), the IMF routinely takes the lead, as in Bulgaria, Guatemala, Russia, and Uganda. The Bank has a good manual on tax administration (Gill 2000), but it has not been updated. Only a few regular Bank staff have the appropriate expertise, so consultants have often been used when IMF support was not available.

More contribution from Bank staff has been needed and is beneficial, according to the case studies, when there are tax administration projects, which the IMF does not have the instruments to design, finance, or supervise. Bank staff expertise is very thin in tax administration, as noted in chapter 3, so care is needed to maintain it and perhaps deepen it.

Anticorruption and transparency

What was the support for ACT trying to achieve? The Bank's standard definition of corruption has been "the abuse of public office for private gain" (World Bank 1997a). Although this does not include all kinds of corruption, it matches well the corruption concerns for reform of the core public sector.

The attention to anticorruption and transparency in CASs, AAA, and projects has grown strongly since the late 1990s, when the "C word" first gained official usage. Initially, corruption only appeared in the CASs of countries that were enthusiastic reformers or that were heavily aid dependent. It was prominent in the 1997 Indonesia CAS and included in the 1998 Honduras and Bolivia CASs. It has become standard in PRSCs, starting with the first in Uganda.

As more countries have opened up on the topic, it has become a negative point of note if a country does not say it is doing something about corruption. Even the most ardent opponents of discussing the topic initially now have something on it in their CASs or Country Partnership Strategy. Real action has come more slowly. The Bank and others usually distinguish two broad types of corruption—state capture (or grand) and bureaucratic (or petty) corruption—and two ways of combating it—indirect and direct—as laid out in table 5.4, showing some examples in each of the categories.

State capture gets the front-page headlines: "Hundreds of millions stolen and stashed overseas" or "Public enterprises sold to insiders for 20 percent of true value." It also includes more subtle examples, where persons with political authority make decisions, without explicit bribes, that ad-

Table 5.4: State Capture and Bureaucratic Corruption, and Indirect Ways to Combat Them

	Types of corruption	
	State capture	**Bureaucratic**
Examples	• Corrupt award of big contracts • Embezzlement of public funds • Kickbacks from big international corporations • Privatization to insiders at bargain prices	• Bribe taking or extraction • Skimming paychecks • Nepotism in appointments • Selective enforcement of taxes • Absentee employees, teachers, doctors • Doctors using public facilities for private paying patients • Teachers tutoring for pay to prepare students for tests
Ways to combat		

Indirect	Transparency
	• Publication of budgets and actual spending—with comprehensible formats
	• Access-to-information law
	• EITI
	• Independent audits published
	• Procurement reform
	    Publication of opportunities
	    Competitive bidding
	    E-procurement
		• Civil service pay reform
		• Expenditure tracking surveys
		• Bank payment systems for taxes and public salaries
		• Public announcement of hiring opportunities
		• Removal of ambiguity from laws and regulations

Direct	• Anticorruption commission with high power • Public officials' disclosure of assets • Investigation and prosecution of officials' unaccounted-for wealth • Stolen asset recovery	• Anticorruption commission with low-level mandate • Prosecution/fining/firing of bribe takers • Code of conduct for public officials • Public officials' disclosure of assets • Investigation and prosecution of officials' unaccounted-for wealth

Source: IEG assessment.

Note: EITI = Extractive Industries Transparency Initiative.

vance the particular interests of their family and business associates.

Bureaucratic corruption usually gets less media attention but can have serious impacts on development: some teachers and doctors frequently fail to come to work, without consequences. People have to pay bribes to get birth certificates or access other public services.

The two phenomena have intrinsic links, however. Costs of grand corruption are described in terms of how many school books and medicine doses the stolen millions would buy, and these calculations assume that efficient noncorrupt institutions use the funds—that is, without much bureaucratic corruption. Grand corruption is rightly condemned for setting a bad example at the top, but the "little guys" at the bottom would tolerate it less if they were not also getting some morsels from petty corruption.

In considering the outcomes for anticorruption and transparency efforts, one must keep in mind that there are many aspects of the anticorruption agenda that are not considered here—such as legal and judicial systems, public utilities, and private corporations—and that CPIA 16 considers not only the ultimate objective of lower corruption but also transparency and accountability. Both are process inputs for reducing corruption, as well as for other objectives.

As shown in table 5.1, only 53 percent of countries getting PSR lending showed improvement in CPIA 16, but the difference between IDA and IBRD borrowers is the largest of any theme. The IDA countries that borrowed for PSR did little better than those that did not. IBRD countries, in contrast, had a 61 percent improvement rate, almost as good as for PFM. Europe and Central Asia had the strongest performance, with 79 percent of borrowers improving, compared with none of the nonborrowers. In half of the Europe and Central Asia countries that borrowed for PSR, CPIA 16 improved by 1.0 or more during the period 1999–2006.

Although many countries now talk about corruption, action has been slow. Other indicators round out this picture. With the Corruption Perception Index (from Transparency International) and the Worldwide Governance Indicator for Control of Corruption (from WBI), about half of the countries getting PSR lending improved their corruption ranking from 1999 to 2006, which is only 4 and 10 percentage points, respectively, better than the countries with no PSR lending.[13]

For IDA countries, the improvement is slightly less, and there is no difference from countries without PSR lending. Because these results are based on rankings, they change at least a little even if nothing changes in the country's performance. The small or zero difference with nonborrowers implies no significant improvement. With the ICRG rating on corruption, the percent of PSR borrowers that improve is much *In some of the case study countries, reforms on other public sector themes improved transparency and reduced bureaucratic corruption.* lower—only 13 percent—and only 2 percent of countries without PSR lending show improvement. These results from the non-CPIA indicators are consistent with results in most of the case studies—there is improved transparency, which explains the improved

CPIA 16, but not usually reduction in corruption per se.

As with civil service reform, reducing corruption involves deeper and more politically challenging change than in PFM. Even today's relatively low corruption in upper-income countries did not come about quickly, but often took generations. Bank programs can have only marginal effects on whether and when the political will materializes to address corruption. The Bank's lending support for anticorruption efforts has mostly used indirect methods, which still predominate, often through reforms to PFM, civil service, and tax administration, as discussed above.

Reducing opportunities for corruption by simplifying procedures and regulations and getting incentives right through, for instance, personnel remuneration schemes, are systemic approaches that have been incorporated in Bank support to PFM, tax administration, and civil service reform. The expressed objectives have been to make public institutions more efficient, transparent, and accountable—all goals valuable in their own right that also contribute to reducing corruption. Some empirical evidence supports the latter connection, although some of the better government effectiveness is explained by higher income, which also correlates with both variables (Kaufmann, Kraay, and Mastruzzi 2005; Islam 2003).

In a variety of places examined for this evaluation—Bulgaria, Guatemala, Indian states such as Andhra Pradesh, Indonesia, Russia, and Tanzania—improvements to PFM (sometimes including implementation of PEFA) and tax administration improved transparency and reduced bureaucratic corruption. State capture has been more difficult to address, and the evaluation did not find clear evidence of success in the cases examined, at least not in the time observed. A sample of HIPC countries that have implemented PEFA showed a similar pattern; the CPIA transparency and corruption indicator (16) has not improved for the majority of the countries (all received PSR lending), even though a majority of the PEFA indicators showed improvement relative to the previous (HIPC) assessment.

Why did the Bank-supported ACT programs achieve as much as they have? Why has there not been more progress? Three groups of issues seem relevant: diagnosis and analysis (AAA), indirect versus direct approaches to different levels of corruption (state capture or bureaucratic), and supply-side versus demand-side approaches.

AAA. Anticorruption and transparency diagnosis and monitoring has been a major growth industry within and outside the Bank for the past decade (Levy 2007; World Bank 2006c). Some of this work, like the World Governance Indicators (from the WBI), tells about aggregate perceptions of the quality of governance in a country. These indicators have served to alert authorities that there is some problem; they can show medium-term results if things improve through government efforts or other factors, but they do not connect to what the government controls directly. Thus, they are not actionable. Some indicators, such as the Doing Business reports, tell about governance issues facing private investors.

BEEPS gathers data about actual government practices toward the companies surveyed, and these are, therefore, actionable indicators for constructing a business-friendly environment.[14] BEEPS was conducted in 2000, 2004, and 2006, and the changes over the period show a record of improvement in PSR borrowers, similar to that from CPIA 16. BEEPS does not cover many aspects of public sector corruption, because of its focus on business issues. That focus, however, is important for attracting foreign investment and therefore getting the attention of political leaders.

In 19 countries, the WBI has done extensive governance diagnostic studies, with much attention given to anticorruption and transparency.[15] WBI diagnostics in Ghana and Guatemala, among the case study countries, were central to developing extensive anticorruption strategies. The diagnostic is a potentially important tool for unbundling corruption, identifying weak/strong institutions, and assessing the costs of corruption on different stakeholders. Moreover, it identifies key determinants of good governance in a number of countries. This WBI governance di-

agnostic also addresses the importance of providing information as a monitoring tool, as well as a tool for empowering stakeholders. Monitoring and follow-up to the diagnostics have often not happened, with exceptions that include Paraguay.

The development and use of diagnostic tools has helped identify potential problem areas.

Although there is no PEFA indicator for corruption, improvements in the 28 areas covered by PEFA can help reduce opportunities for corruption. Most CPARs and CFAAs do not adequately address the question of how well procurement and financial management systems protect against or reduce the risk of corruption. They do not discuss specific methods to identify corrupt practices and measures to deter them in procurement and financial management. They rarely look at the incentives for corruption in these areas. A few have done so, such as for Bolivia and Indonesia, and with broader application this could help countries reduce corruption (IEG 2007).

For instance, researchers in Italy have developed a method to measure corruption by comparing the growth of infrastructure stock with amounts of spending. In the context of Bank work this would also identify the project areas where corruption is draining off the most public investment resources (Golden and Picci 2005).

The World Bank has been instrumental in developing new tools that help improve transparency and societal accountability, such as the PETS in 13 countries and quantitative service delivery surveys in FYR Macedonia and Papua New Guinea (DFID n.d.). Although some of the instruments used by the Bank and bilateral donors to assess fiduciary risk have been useful for identifying institutional weaknesses in the PFM systems of developing countries, especially the PEFA framework, the absence of political and cultural factors in these analyses reflects a general weakness in Bank and donor approaches to anticorruption.

Indirect or direct approaches for different levels of corruption. Many of the previously mentioned reforms to PFM, civil service (recruitment and pay reform), and tax administration are

Box 5.2: Extractive Industries Transparency Initiative–Multi-Donor Trust Fund

Thus far, 22 developing countries have signed on to the Extractive Industries Transparency Initiative (EITI)—14 in Africa, 3 in Europe and Central Asia, 2 in East Asia, and 3 in Latin America and the Caribbean.

To help countries implement the principles, the Multi-Donor Trust Fund for the EITI was established in 2004 through an agreement between DFID and the World Bank. The governments of Germany, the Netherlands, and Norway joined in 2005. The goal of the EITI–Multi-Donor Trust Fund is to broaden support for the EITI principles and process by establishing extractive industries transparency initiatives in countries. The Multi-Donor Trust Fund is an arrangement whereby the Bank manages funds on behalf of multiple donors.

The EITI–Multi-Donor Trust Fund currently funds activities in more than 12 countries, and the EITI has been endorsed in almost 10 more. Country-specific grant agreements are signed between the recipient country and the Bank to define and establish which activities are to be executed by the recipient.

Source: EITI Web site (http://www.eitransparency.org).

important indirect ways to reduce bureaucratic corruption by reducing opportunities and incentives for corrupt acts. Increasing transparency and access to information in all parts of the public sector also help reduce state capture by supplying information that the media, civil society, and the broader political process can use to demand accountability and uncorrupt behavior from political leaders. Support for these measures has been the most important way to date that the Bank has advanced the anticorruption effort. Examples include the civil service, procurement, financial management, and tax administration measures in Albania, Bolivia, Guatemala, Russia, and the Republic of Yemen.

Against state-capture corruption, the Extractive Industries Transparency Initiative (EITI) has received Bank support for the international set-up and for implementation in at least 12 of the 22 developing countries that have signed on (box 5.2). EITI improves transparency on the revenue side, but its potential and hoped-for effects in reducing corruption and increasing transparency in the use of funds depend mainly on a

Reforms to financial management, civil service, and tax administration are important indirect approaches to reducing the potential for corruption.

process of information about mineral revenues stimulating domestic political demands for accountability and for more information. If a country already has the infrastructure of inquisitive media, opposition parties, and democratic budgeting, EITI could have good effects on transparency and corruption in a few years. In most of the EITI signatory countries where the Bank has provided support, however, there are great needs for institution building.[16]

Direct anticorruption efforts supported by the Bank have mostly targeted bureaucratic corruption, such as an anticorruption commission with low-level mandate, prosecution and firing of those who take bribes, establishing a code of conduct for public officials, requiring public officials to disclose their assets, and investigation and prosecution of officials' unaccounted wealth. In Guatemala, however, the government showed only limited support for strengthening the anticorruption commission, even as it supported measures—computerized systems for financial management information and procurement—that indirectly reduced corruption.

Most of these direct anticorruption mechanisms also have potential against senior politicians and businessmen involved in state capture, but they are rarely invoked except to settle political scores. In Indian states, the anticorruption commissions—some of which are supported in Bank operations—usually can investigate officials above a certain level only with permission of the head of the administration. The issue illustrates the difficult balance between protecting officials from politically motivated prosecution and making sure that all are subject to anticorruption rules. In Ghana, the Commission on Human Rights and Administrative Justice has a small anticorruption unit cofunded by the government and donor; it has reported that the government has restrained its work and independence.

Tanzania had a good enquiry (United Republic of Tanzania 1996) into forms, loci, causes, and remedies for corruption. Its main recommendation was to treat the problem of corruption by starting at the top, but the government has not implemented the recommendations. The Good Governance Coordination Unit (donor funded but staffed with Tanzanian civil servants) and the Prevention and Combating of Corruption Bureau have not done much yet. The national anticorruption strategy and action plan theoretically empowers private citizens to take up a corruption issue, but none seems to have done this with any effect. Although the plan seems an ambitious and all-encompassing anticorruption approach, it lacks serious mechanisms to monitor compliance or to hold implementing agencies accountable. Indirect anticorruption efforts through financial management have been more effective through the Ministry of Finance and the Public Procurement Regulatory Authority. Support to the National Audit Office has also encouraged demand-side transparency.

The Bank's country strategy and major operations have directly addressed state-capture corruption only in rare cases, when deep political and economic crises exposed the corruption of old regimes and brought in new ones dedicated to a fresh start, such as in Indonesia in the late 1990s and Nigeria after 2003. Advocating wholesale transformation of neopatrimonial governments has been politically difficult for the Bank and is usually avoided, even when formal or informal analytic work identifies the problem, as it did in Bangladesh, Bolivia, Peru, and the Philippines.

Focusing reform efforts on combatting bureaucratic corruption seems unfair if state-capture corruption is persisting, but it may serve to make public service delivery more efficient and helpful to citizens while staying within the bounds of political feasibility. Reducing state capture (if possible) would make reduction of bureaucratic corruption more effective and sustainable, and reducing bureaucratic corruption seems to have some use in itself and may help move the broader political culture toward opposing grand corruption. In perception-based indicators of corruption, however, the persistence of state capture may obscure progress in fighting bureaucratic corruption.

Supply- and demand-side approaches. The measures discussed above are in the supply-side

category, in that the reforms are supplied by the government (perhaps in response to domestic or international demands) and address corrupt practices by the government (perhaps in response to bribes that accompany private sector demands). In its transparency and anticorruption efforts (like the rest of PRS), the Bank has focused mainly on the supply side, because it generally works with governments and needs those governments' approval for its activities.

Direct anticorruption efforts supported by the Bank have mostly targeted bureaucratic corruption.

Nonetheless, there are more than a dozen projects listed in the GAC (World Bank 2007c) with components aimed specifically at the demand side for PSR in the areas of this evaluation. Most of them include measures to strengthen the oversight capacity of legislatures and their audit committees. Other support for the demand side includes WBI courses and contact with civil society, the media, and NGOs. Some programs, for example, in Guatemala and Indonesia, include measures to strengthen grassroots monitoring of local infrastructure developments and assist the media in enhancing transparency. Transparency and accountability of the budget processes are also reflected in some country portfolios, such as in Uganda. Generally, however, supply-side factors are at the core of the Bank's support of anticorruption. In particular, this applies to support to improve PFM legislation, public procurement systems, capacity of the auditor general's office, and CSA, especially payroll reforms.

Increasing awareness of the potential role of civil society in fighting corruption has only materialized in a few of the Bank's anticorruption lending programs. For example, reforms in Ghana to strengthen good governance and social accountability have to an important extent been demand driven from civil society; the Freedom of Information Act is expected to further strengthen the voice of civil society. In Indonesia, demand-side efforts brought in civil society and local stakeholders to perform monitoring and evaluation functions, especially in decentralization projects, investment climate surveys, and PETS.

Country strategies and Bank operations have rarely addressed state capture directly.

In Ukraine, the Bank has supported a program called Voices of the People. This program's goal is to improve municipal-level integrity by strengthening the voice of citizen groups as they demand better services and governance. The Canadian International Development Agency also supported this program. It started as a pilot in four cities, monitoring local service delivery, promoting NGO capacity, and facilitating public involvement in government decision making. Positive reaction to the first phase led to the addition of six more cities for the second phase, starting in 2003.

The persistence of state capture may obscure progress in fighting bureaucratic corruption.

The cases and literature reviewed raise challenges to traditional supply-side approaches—leaving it to the government and a country's legal institutions to devise and enforce public accountability. Conventional mechanisms, such as anticorruption commissions and audit and legislative reviews, may not be enough (Reinikka and Svensson 2006, p. 368). Collusion, organizational deficiencies, abuse of power, and lack of responsiveness to citizens have been hard to detect and rectify, even with the best of supervision. When the institutions are weak, as is common in developing countries, the government's potential role as auditor and supervisor is even more constrained.

Evidence suggests that corruption can be substantially reduced only when the supply-side reforms are complemented by systematic efforts to increase the citizens' capability to monitor and challenge abuses of the system and to inform the citizens about their rights and entitlements. Breaking the culture of secrecy that pervades the government functioning and empowering people to demand public accountability are important components in such an effort.

Tailoring an anticorruption strategy to country circumstances. The Bank dutifully repeats the mantra of "no one size fits all," yet it has not developed guidance on what to do if the Chilean or Nordic size—that is, the size that fits most countries where the Bank lends—does not come close to fitting in the country at hand, especially IDA countries. Most developing countries today (as with Western Europe and the United States 150 years ago) have political systems that depend fundamentally on patronage. In these places the recommendation *to be opportunistic* in fighting all types of corruption often degenerates into a game, where prosecuting corruption when it becomes most obvious or politically vulnerable leads to it popping out elsewhere. An open dialogue about the realistic options is needed.

The typologies of corruption elaborated above still do not provide a way to assess the cost of different corruption types to development, set the corresponding priorities, and choose remedies that work for the relevant situations.[17] The experiences in Indonesia, Nigeria, and Russia suggest that reducing the development cost of corruption is a politically attainable goal, even where patronage is ingrained in the political system. Even in patronage-based, corrupt governments, most leaders want to have at least somewhat more and better public services and infrastructure in return for their patronage spending. Beyond keeping corruption out of the projects it finances (which should be a high priority because the projects are presumably of high value for development), the Bank has not developed a systematic way to determine how it can and should work in such situations.

Summary Lessons from Thematic Comparisons

Standards and measurements

Actionable indicators exist for PFM and tax administration. Indicators exist for corruption perception, but mostly they are not actionable. Indicators for transparency are being developed in some areas—such as the Open Budget Project—and could be replicated in others. These indicators have sometimes been used to define project objectives and baselines, but this could be done more systematically. That would give more objective indicators for judging project outcomes, rather than relative to objectives defined in terms unique to each project, as is now the case with almost all projects.

For civil service, a few indicators exist, such as number of public employees, wage bills, dispersion ratios for wage rates, and (occasionally) absenteeism. However, these are not widely or systematically tracked. Also there is not a set of internationally standardized indicators established within a coherent framework for analysis.

Core agenda to be adapted
Everyone agrees that one size does not fit all, but it also seems important to start with a basic adaptable pattern and from that learn the best ways to adapt it. PFM, transparency of budget, and tax administration have such patterns, which the Bank, the IMF, OECD, and various other agencies and bilaterals have helped develop.

For civil service and administration, there is no such a pattern, although the beginnings for it have been tried in isolated instances. Where management of civil service and other personnel is weak, the Bank has had some successes in supporting the gathering of reliable data on numbers, total compensation, and attendance and the institutionalization of these processes. Improving the links between personnel management and financial management information systems has also been a useful way to get a technocratic start on problems that are often highly politicized.

Motivation and competence of counterparts
In PFM and tax administration, a lot of project, AAA, and IDF resources go to capacity building in the counterpart agencies. In the areas of CSA re-

form, there is less clarity about what content should be. Capacity building needs to include not only technical skills but also skills in managing and monitoring people.

Interdependence of the thematic areas
The analysis of PSR by themes should not leave the impression that they can or should be dealt with in isolation. There is a particular temptation to leave civil service out, as out of fashion or too difficult in practice, although it is sometimes also dismissed as "easy, if there is only the political will." Nonetheless, CSA reform affects the incentives and capacities of the people who have to implement reforms in all the other areas, so it cannot be ignored.

In the CPIA, the ratings for PFM are usually better than for CSA, but never by more than one grade (except in one country that has 5.5 for PFM and 4.0 for CSA). Improving PFM to the point where it gets beyond just processes and has real effects on public service performance and accountability has not happened without also improving the civil service.

The extent of coordination among Bank staff specializing in the themes discussed here varies within the operational Regions. Country cases and other staff interviews revealed that in (large) country offices, where the specialists sit in proximity, and in Latin America and the Caribbean, with country management teams representing all the areas, there tends to be better coordination. In other contexts, the Bank has not developed adequate institutions to avoid having silos in the Bank reflect and reinforce those that exist in the client countries.

Chapter 6

Parliment building in Cape Town, South Africa. Photo by Trevor Samson, courtesy of World Bank Photo Library.

Strategic Summary, Ratings, and Recommendations

The motivation of countries for PSR has varied widely and mostly has involved factors beyond the control of the World Bank Group. Awareness of the motives is important for the Bank to choose the appropriate instruments.

Reform Motivations, Expectations, and Success Factors

Popular pressure and the desire for faster economic growth and improved public services frequently motivate reform. In countries with well-established democratic processes and a free press, such as Mexico, Costa Rica, Chile, India, and the Czech Republic, the demand for PSR has been substantial.

The Bank has sometimes played an encouraging role by fueling the demand with information, working with local think tanks and academic institutions, and supporting special institutions, such as Mexico's Federal Institute for Access to Information. Participatory PERs in Tanzania, Uganda, and Vietnam that the World Bank supports have increased the popular interest in public expenditure and whetted the appetite for more information, especially in local think tanks and NGOs. But these types of PERs are still not common.

A ***fiscal crisis*** has frequently motivated countries to seek support from the Bank and other donors for PSR, especially if financial assistance is expected. Among the four areas of PSR discussed here, tax administration and basic financial management have been most frequently what the government was eager to do as a remedy for fiscal crisis. Actual and potential taxpayers suffer in a fiscal crisis, so they are then more likely to support better revenue collection. South Korean businessmen were explicit about this in 1998, as they increased voluntary tax compliance to help the country during the financial crisis. The Ministry of Finance, the World Bank Group's typical counterpart, is motivated to see reforms in these areas and is the typical agent for accomplishing them.

So the fiscal crisis motivation most often leads to tax administration and PFM as entry points (Russia, Tanzania, Colombia, Indian states, and Argentina). In rare cases, the government has successfully used civil service retrenchment as a fiscal development policy measure (Tanzania and some Indian states), but more often this does not go beyond temporary freezes on salaries and hiring. Fiscal crises are almost always temporary, so except as memories they do not sustain the motivation that is needed for more complex reforms that take longer to implement.

European Union accession has also successfully motivated PSR, and the positive results are striking. Other factors may also have contributed to these positive outcomes, such as completing the dual transitions to democracy and from state-planned to market economies. The governance CPIA ratings for the 10 accession countries have almost all improved since 1999.[1]

Although this specific model is not replicable in most other parts of the world, three features of the situation of the European Union accession countries have general lessons. First, the European Union's conditions for entry are comprehensive and standardized, with the pre-announced rewards (accession and major funding) dependent on the extent and pace with which the country meets the standards. Second, the promise of rewards and enforcement of standards are both highly credible and extend over a long period—forever on the issue of admission. Third, the European Union–accession scenario enhanced the World Bank's effectiveness by emphasizing its role as an advisor and facilitator, not an arm twister, and its relatively small financing for PSR had importance mainly through the earmark of money for technical assistance and the supervision process.

A fourth category of motivation, and one over which the Bank has considerable control, is **_financial support,_** which includes general budget support through loans, credits (IDA loans), grants, debt relief (HIPC), and investment loans for the costs of specific PSR activities. Budget support often carries high hopes as a motivator, but four realities have limited the effectiveness of financial support as motivation for reform:

• First, countries where the Bank has the most financial leverage have the furthest to go to improve institutions, but the weakest capacity to implement change. Countries with strong institutional capacity to implement change, in contrast, are also likely to have good access to financial markets and are thus less motivated by the attractiveness of Bank financing. Indeed, some see the acceptance of Bank financing as the price to pay for getting the expertise that comes with the money—a price these countries are still willing to pay.

• Second, the Bank is often the leader of a concert of donors, which adds to the financial leverage but also makes the demands more diverse and less focused, as each donor has its own set of priorities. The Bank has helped coordinate these demands—sometimes at a government's request—with varying degrees of success. In Tanzania and Guyana, this went relatively well, but in other cases—Bangladesh and Honduras—multiple agendas led to overly complex sets of conditions.

• Third, the Bank may find itself under pressure to lend for various reasons—international political strategy, defensive lending to avert default, or the momentum of delivering budget support on a predictable annual cycle. It has sometimes done this despite PSR conditions that are vague or not well enforced, as a way to justify the lending. This type of lending undermines the credibility the World Bank's seal of approval for PSR programs.

• Fourth, the Bank's tight schedules for commitment and disbursement of lending, especially for IDA, often conflict with the long period typically needed to implement PSR and the need to respect political cycles and build consensus and capacity. Investment projects did better in this regard, especially if they were adaptable program loans, like the public service reform loan in Tanzania. These relatively small investment projects were useful as a financial incentive to the implementing agency, but not for political ownership by the government as a whole. Consequently, the most effective PSR support from the Bank has often come in situations where the country does not urgently need lending.

Expectations for the progress and effects of PSR are the foundations for motivating the government to undertake them and the Bank and other donors to finance them. Thus, the ideal balance is for expectations to be high enough to motivate but not so high that they misguide efforts or that failures to meet them erode credibility and commitment. Expectations for PSR have often been unrealistic. Some of this is due to overstated goals and the mismatch of objectives with disbursement timelines. The generic problem was recognized at least as early as the 1992 Wapenhans report (World Bank 1992a), and the programmatic development policy (now, development policy) loans and adaptable program loans were introduced as instruments to allow longer time horizons.[2]

Nonetheless, the momentum of high budget-support programs encouraged the search for success stories that were sometimes overhyped and led to overstated objectives, at least in the period under evaluation. Thus, compared to middle-income countries that pay essentially the full market rate for loans, the pressure to exaggerate was greater for the IDA countries, which faced if anything greater challenges to produce results in the short and medium term.

Expectations about reforming civil service and reducing corruption have been especially difficult to manage. Successful reforms in these areas have taken a long time in any country, with important historical antecedents. Although the Bank dutifully repeats the mantra of "no one size fits all," it has not developed guidance on what pace of progress to expect, given the initial conditions in a country. Most developing countries today (such as Western Europe and the United States 150 years ago) have political systems that depend fundamentally on patronage. Some countries have progressed more quickly in recent years, but an open dialogue about the realistic expectations has been missing.

Country PSR Strategy Entry Points

In concluding, there are two cross-cutting questions: First, what should be the scope of reforms? Second, what is the best mix of policy-based and investment lending?

There are continuing debates over whether reforms should be rapid and comprehensive in scope, taking a "big bang" approach, or incremental and opportunistic (Wescott 2006). Some stress the need for a "top-down," politically driven, all-encompassing reform process to take advantage of narrow windows of opportunity. In contrast, North views piecemeal reforms as more

typical: "The single most important point about institutional change, which must be grasped if we are to begin to get a handle on the subject, is that institutional change is overwhelmingly incremental" (North 1990, p. 89). Although there would seem to be more evidence of success of incremental rather than strategy-driven reform, both types have worked at times, and both have sometimes failed.

One pattern we do see is that rapid reform only succeeds when there is strong support at the beginning—European Union accession countries are the best group of cases—whereas gradual reforms have sometimes succeeded when public support was initially weak (but did exist), because early successes of reform pilots builds support for more.

With either pattern of reforms, it has been useful for the Bank to get a comprehensive and politically savvy overview and strategy at the beginning, which then gets modified as events unfold. This need not be formal ESW, publicly disseminated. Sometimes a background paper on sensitive political issues can be presented as research in an academic setting, with a government representative as discussant; the Bank then need not take an official position. The case studies show that with governments unsure about doing PSR, focused and technocratic AAA (not necessarily formal ESW) has often opened the door for wider dialogue and eventually for lending support for PSR.

The Bank and its borrowing partners have tried a variety of combinations of investment lending and development policy lending, including for the support of PSR. Investment and technical assistance lending by itself can work well when the government has the appropriate policy and legal framework in place and the implementing agency has good motivation, institutional autonomy, and clear access to the funds. This is more likely to prevail in middle-income countries and more modern Indian states. Where the appropriate policy framework and incentives are not in place, an investment loan will not generate them, even with a willing implementing agency, as in Venezuela and Argentina.

Where the country is getting substantial Provincial Reform Loan or PRSC funds, the Bank and other development partners often have assumed that governments will give adequate resources and attention to implementing institutional reforms, but this has not always happened, as seen in Uganda and Bangladesh (see IDD & Associates 2006). In such cases, the big but not always reliable inflows of budget support go to the large high-priority areas, such as education and health; this is appropriate, but the details of implementing new systems of financial management or personnel administration get bypassed.

However, in other cases, channeling aid through country systems has strengthened budget processes, including comprehensiveness and transparency. In cases where there is a multiyear investment technical assistance loan, especially an adaptable program loan, then the agency managing the project gets funds as needed for implementation but also gets the long-term and focused attention of the supervision team, which may help to improve fiduciary systems.

Summary Evaluation Ratings

To arrive at summary ratings, the evaluation builds up from ratings in each of the four themes and differentiates AAA and funding operations. Because the borrower performance and outcome are so heterogeneous and largely beyond the Bank's control, the ratings here are for Bank performance

as a way to focus the learning process. Nonetheless, the country outcomes carry over somewhat to the ratings of Bank performance, as it contributes to outcomes.

For every cell of the resulting 2×5 matrix, shown in table 6.1, there are examples of highly satisfactory work. So the results reflect the median, based mainly on the tasks that were done but also considering opportunities missed. Almost every borrower country needed some support in every cell of the matrix. Sometimes other development partners covered part of the program, so the Bank played a lesser role there and in some cases played none. In every case the Bank and country authorities (and often other development partners) share the credit or blame for the outcomes, with the Bank having more control and therefore more responsibility for the AAA and the countries having more control over the selection, design, and especially outcomes in the project areas.

The ratings here focus on Bank performance, particularly the more strategic aspects of setting agendas, fostering synergies within country portfolios, and allocating and organizing Bank resources. Thus, the ratings here differ from those for individual PSR projects, which are usually rated satisfactory for Bank performance.

In the PFM area, the diagnostics have developed strongly, especially since 2000, with PEFA and Public Expenditure and Institutional Reviews being highly satisfactory examples. In most cases, the Bank offered well-structured packages of lending

Table 6.1: Overall Bank Performance Ratings, 1999–2006

Reform area	AAA	Lending
Public expenditure and financial management	Highly satisfactory	Moderately satisfactory
Civil service and administration	Unsatisfactory	Moderately unsatisfactory
Tax administration	N.A. (IMF usually leads)	Satisfactory
Direct anticorruption and transparency	Moderately unsatisfactory	Moderately unsatisfactory
Integration and consistency across themes	Moderately unsatisfactory	Moderately unsatisfactory
Overall	Moderately satisfactory	

Source: IEG assessment.

Note: AAA = analytical and advisory activities; IMF = International Monetary Fund.

support, although sometimes the packages were overly complex or gave too little attention to behavioral aspects of institutional change. Government ownership for PFM investment projects was usually good, because the main counterparts—the ministries of finance—have a clear interest in such projects. Implementation of the budget—procurement and financial management—still has received too little attention, especially in policy reform lending projects. The set-up of Bank projects with PIUs and ring fencing has sometimes hindered improvement in financial management of the rest of the country's resources.

For civil service, there has been some improvement in the decade since the previous IEG evaluation, but not enough. Although some projects have followed and had success with incremental approaches that emphasize improving personnel management, in other places the Bank (often with the IMF) continued to support simplistic retrenchment programs of the same sort that failed in the past. Too often CSA diagnostic AAA is simply not done before projects tackle reform, as in 8 of 18 case study countries. The absence of a good analytic and diagnostic framework hinders both AAA and projects for CSA reform. Promising pilots in a few countries have not been replicated widely or brought into a multiagency context to build international consensus for the equivalent of PEFA. Analysis and projects do not focus often enough on the features that would do the most to improve the quality and efficiency of service delivery, although there has been some movement in that direction.

Tax administration, the smallest area of Bank activity in the PSR field, illustrates the potential for reform when there is a good diagnostic and reform framework (typically led by the IMF) combined with typically enthusiastic government support and effective project management from the Bank.

Anticorruption and transparency is new as an area of its own. The Bank has done a lot of survey work that contributes to anticorruption diagnosis, especially to improve the environment for business (as with BEEPS), but there has been less diagnostic work at the country level about corruption in the core PSM areas that are the focus of this report. The CPAR and CFAA, for instance, have not usually given much attention to corruption issues pertaining to procurement and financial management. The requisite analysis of political factors in the specific country contexts was typically missing.

Even more than in other areas, top-level government ownership is essential for making progress against corruption, but the diagnostic work and program design rarely took this into account. Furthermore, adequate guidelines for how to do this did not exist, even in the 2007 GAC strategy. (The learning process under way for its implementation aims to address this, but it is beyond the scope of this evaluation.)

Because the main themes of PSR—PFM, civil service, and anticorruption—look at different sides of essentially the same phenomenon, the whole portfolio of Bank support for PSR should be greater than the sum of the parts. But it is less. Coordination and integration across the themes has often been inadequate or lacking, although this improved in some country programs during the evaluation period. The country GAC strategies, now being developed as pilots, offer an opportunity to address this shortcoming more systematically.

The overall rating for Bank performance is *moderately satisfactory*, although the picture is heterogeneous. PFM has been the largest area of Bank activity for PSR, and performance there has been moderately to highly satisfactory. This outweighs the shortcomings in other areas.

Recommendations

There are many favorable trends in PSR that the Bank should continue to pursue and many areas where improvements are needed. This chapter highlights three recommendations.

Recognize the complexity and political nature of PSR

First, the design of PSR projects and resource allocation to them needs to reflect the fact that they face more complex political and sequencing issues than in most traditional areas of the Bank's activity. This implies, therefore, the need to (i) set project objectives with realistic recognition of the time it takes to get significant results, (ii) understand the political context, identifying prerequisites to achieve the objectives, and (iii) focus first on the basic reforms that a country needs in its initial situation and that generate political support for the process.

The PEFA indicators provide a good basis for this in the PFM area, because they will track incremental progress. As institutional change needs sustained support, that support usually needs to include investment projects; although development policy lending can help secure the enabling policy changes, it is not generally a substitute for investment loans.

The political complexity and typically longer duration of public sector reforms mean more analytical and preparatory work, including on political issues. They also mean that any one loan, especially fast disbursing, will promise more modest, incremental progress. For some countries, these changes may entail more loans per year. Investment loans will often need to have longer duration. This does not mean to stop encouraging a government to progress as fast as possible, but it does recognize the value in setting more realistic targets that, when accomplished, will enhance the credibility of public sector reform in that country and more generally.

These considerations are especially relevant for countries starting with weaker-than-average capacity, and the initial steps there may need to focus on capacity building and data collection. Countries with severe governance problems, where the "bottom billion" live, may need more AAA for PSR—nonlending technical assistance as well as formal ESW—prior to policy reform lending.

Prioritize PSR efforts

Second, devote more effort at both country and thematic levels to identify in each country where PSR—including anticorruption efforts—will contribute most to poverty reduction and growth. This would feed into the country GACs mandated by the 2007 GAC. Based on this, the country teams would clarify the sequencing and priorities with which they would be addressing the long-term agenda of reducing corruption and improving other aspects of governance.

Enabling such diagnosis at the country level may require a strategic framework from the center. The country team might meet as a group to compare and synthesize knowledge about areas where corruption is a problem. Comparing cost of corruption across all sectors may not be possible in the near term, but the country GACs could include AAA to assess the costs of corruption within specific areas that previous information (Worldwide Governance Indicators, CPIA, CPARs) identifies as problematic—such as business licensing, procurement, and tax administration.

For instance, researchers in Italy have developed a method to measure corruption by comparing the growth of infrastructure stock with amounts of spending, which in the context of Bank work would also identify the project areas where corruption is draining off the most public investment resources (Golden and Picci 2005). The Bank's diagnostic work looks comparatively at corruption costs to some extent already, as in Doing Business and BEEPS. The recommendation is to do this more systematically, aiming at comparability. An alternative approach could look comprehensively at all areas (procurement, human resources management, taxation, licensing and regulation, and so forth) of one or more sectors identified as pivotal for that country—such as natural resource management, health, or agriculture.

To complement estimates of the cost of corruption, institutional and political analysis (perhaps in the Institutional Governance Review format) would need to consider the cost and feasibility of the measures that aim to reduce the most costly types of corruption. Having zero tolerance for corruption in Bank-financed investment projects makes sense in light of their high value for development (that is why the Bank finances them) and the strong institutional mechanisms that are available to fight corruption in these projects. These justifications from the country point of view are in addition to the rationale of protecting the anticorruption reputation of the Bank.

To reduce the negative effect of corruption on growth and poverty reduction, Bank support for PSR should emphasize (i) building systems (in areas such as PFM, procurement, tax administration, and human resources management and information systems, as well as in licensing and registration services, social services, and so on) that reduce the opportunities for corruption that is most costly to development (including any that might be in Bank-supported projects) and (ii) making better information public (as with PETS, EITI, publicly discussed PERs, citizen report cards, and so forth) in ways that stimulate public demand for more efficient and less corrupt service delivery.

Building the capacity of demand-side institutions, like the legislature and its audit office and the news media, is often needed to complement the measures to improve access to information. Only when the country has both strong political will and an adequate judiciary system should the Bank's support for anticorruption put primary emphasis on anticorruption laws and commissions.

Set a better framework for CSA
Third, keep CSA reforms (including human resources management systems) as a major component of PSR, but design and implement them with a better framework, and give more attention to the budget-execution phases of PFM. Despite the difficulties of improving CSA reform, it is not something that can be ignored. Improving PFM to the point where it gets beyond just processes and has real effects on public service performance and accountability has not happened without also improving the civil service.

A better framework for CSA reform will require things such as elaboration and implementation of a PEFA-like set of actionable indicators for CSA performance, which is foreseen in the 2007 GAC strategy. There may need to be variants corresponding to different types of public administrations—such as presidential, continental European, and Whitehall. These indicators would guide the analysis of CSA issues in CASs/Country Partnership Strategies, as would AAA and lending.

As the framework for CSA diagnosis and reform improves, the Bank's staffing for public management, including the civil service area, may need enhancement in line with its importance in the lending programs. Finding resources for this will face the usual budget constraints, and management may consider shifting some resources out of standard macroeconomic analysis, especially where the Bank's program is relatively small and the IMF already does a lot of analytic work. For instance, the Bank might consider having a political scientist or public management specialist with some macroeconomics background as the core of its team for some small countries.

Segment of mural *El Buen Gobierno* by Diego Rivera (1924). Courtesy of Universidad Autónoma de Chapingo, where this mural appears in the Administration Building.

Appendixes

1. Lending

The lending projects included in this public sector reform (PSR) evaluation were selected through two processes, both looking at projects approved during fiscal years 1990 through 2006. One process (with multiple steps) started with a list of projects from the World Bank project database that had at least 25 percent of the project dedicated to PSR-related *themes* or *sectors*.

PSR-related *themes* in this selection process included administrative and civil service reform; public expenditure, financial management and procurement; tax policy and administration; other accountability/anticorruption; and other public sector governance. PSR-related *sectors* included central government administration, subnational government administration, and general public administration.

The team examined each project's appraisal documentation and included only the projects that had objectives and policy actions pertaining to public budgeting and financial management (including audit and procurement), civil service and administrative reform, tax administration, and anticorruption and transparency.

Some development policy lending included so many sectors and themes that PSR-related shares did not make the 25 percent cutoff, even though there were important PSR conditions. So the team did a second selection process, using the Adjustment Lending Conditionality and Implementation Database. If there were at least three conditions required for loan disbursement as either prior actions or legal tranche-release conditions[1] in the focus areas of the evaluation, then that project was added. Many of these projects were already included from the first process.

The intersection of these two processes comprised 467 projects—the main database for the evaluation. A list of these projects has been included as appendix B (http://www.worldbank.org/ieg/psr/appendix.html). For each project, descriptive information was also collected from an internal database, including a short description, commitment amounts, important dates, sector board, network, project status, lending instrument type, and other information.

Within the data set, the projects were coded to indicate whether they had components in the following four thematic categories: public finance management (PFM), civil service and administrative (CSA) reform, tax administration (TAX), or anticorruption and governance (transparency).

Many of the projects in the database included activities in more than one of these categories. The percentage allocations[2] of all of the themes related to PSR were combined to estimate a combined share of the project allocated to PSR. This number was multiplied by the loan commitment amount to obtain a rough indication of funding (in dollars) allocated to PSR.

2. Analytic and Advisory Activities

The analytic and advisory activities (AAA) list used the following criteria:

(i) Only AAA that was delivered to the client between fiscal 1999 and 2006 is included. Internal databases do not allow retrieving a complete list of AAA prior to fiscal 1999.

(ii) All core reports (Country Economic Memorandum [CEMs]/Development Policy Reviews [DPRs], Public Expenditure Reviews, Country Financial Accountability Assessment, Country Procurement Assessment Reports) were included if they had as their main sector any of the following eight categories: general public administration, central government administration, public sector management, public financial management, civil service reform, other public sector reforms, institutional development, and subnational government.

(iii) For the noncore AAA, the team carefully read the titles of all AAA that were either mapped under four sector boards (Public Sector Governance, Financial Management, Procurement, and Economic Policy) or had as their main sector one of the above eight categories. AAA that had a heavy sectoral focus was excluded from this list.

(iv) For the AAA that did not fall under the above four sector boards or eight sector categories, the team used word-search techniques and added those products relevant to our evaluation. Once the core and noncore lists were complete, the team classified each AAA as PFM, TAX, administrative and civil service, or anticorruption and governance (CEM/DPRs and Public Expenditure Reviews were classified as generic PSR, because these products cover several sectors not captured by the internal Bank database). The total number of AAA projects is 803. This list is in appendix C (http://www.worldbank.org/ieg/psr/appendix.html).

3. Institutional Development Fund grants

The Institutional Development Fund (IDF) list was based on a complete list of active and closed IDFs (which began in fiscal 1992). The team followed a procedure similar to steps (iii) and (iv) for AAA. Team members carefully read the titles of all IDFs that were either mapped under the sector boards Public Sector Governance, Financial Management, Procurement, and Economic Policy, or that had as their main sector one of the eight categories (general public administration, central government administration, public sector management, PFM, civil service reform, other public sector reforms, institutional development, and subnational government). IDFs with a heavy sectoral focus were dropped from this list. For the IDFs not under the above four sector boards or eight sector categories, the team used word-search techniques and added the ones relevant to the evaluation. Once the list was complete, the team classified each IDF as PFM, TAX, CSA, or transparency. The total number of IDFs is 279. Appendix D (http://www.worldbank.org/ieg/psr/appendix.html) lists them.

The Panel believes that the report *Public Sector Reform: What Works and Why?* by the Independent Evaluation Group (IEG) provides a very competent and informative analysis of the Bank's efforts to promote PSR from 1999 to 2006. The importance of good governance to development has been well established in the academic literature at this point; given the large and steadily increasing amount of PSR lending by the Bank, evaluation of the Bank's efforts in this regard is critical.

The history of the Bank's involvement with PSR in the report is very useful, and the four main thematic areas highlighted—public financial management, tax administration, CSA reform, and anticorruption and transparency—cover the most important dimensions of PSR. The report appropriately recognizes the underlying complexity and the challenges posed by PSR and is sensitive to the multivariate and bidirectional nature of causality in government performance. The Panel also commends the three-pronged approach of country case studies, thematic assessments, and statistical analysis as an appropriate methodology for an evaluation in this intrinsically difficult area. The report underlines the importance of performing a broad political economy analysis before proceeding with PSR and the need for the Bank to include more noneconomists on its country teams to help in this effort. We fully endorse this recommendation.

The Panel feels that the report's findings could be strengthened or extended in the following areas:

1. The statistical analysis in chapters 4 and 5 relies very heavily on Country Policy and Institutional Assessments (CPIA) scores. Although the CPIA yardstick may be familiar to people in the Bank, it is not well known outside the Bank (indeed, CPIA scores for middle-income countries are not publicly available). This means that they (unlike, for example, the World Bank Institute Worldwide Governance Indicators) have not been carefully scrutinized externally for possible biases, endogeneity, and so forth. It may well be, as the report suggests, that no better set of indicators exists, but it is worth explaining at greater length how the CPIA scores are derived and their possible weaknesses.

2. As far as the Panel can tell, the statistical analysis is not based on a full-blown multivariate statistical analysis that seeks to isolate the degree of variance in governance outcomes accounted for by Bank PSR programs. It is therefore not possible to know with any reasonable confidence the extent to which improvements in public sector performance result from Bank PSR operations versus other factors, such as the intensity of PSR activities, complementary programs by other donors, or exogenous trends (such as European Union accession). The Panel appreciates that it may not be possible to perform this kind of analysis given the limitations of the data, but more explicit recognition of this problem would have been appropriate.

3. The report makes some scattered allusions to the importance of stimulating demand for good governance, an issue that has been under considerable discussion within the Bank in recent years. However, the conclusions and recommendations make no reference to a possible role for the Bank on the demand side.

4. What is most striking about the report is the finding that public financial management and

tax administration operations have been reasonably effective in improving public sector performance in most Bank client countries, but that civil service reform and anticorruption efforts have not had a significant impact on outcomes. Accordingly, the Panel expected a recommendation that the Bank should focus much more heavily on the relatively technical areas of public financial management and tax administration that it knows best. There is no such recommendation. Somewhat inexplicably, the report recommends that the Bank continue with civil service reform and anticorruption and transparency efforts (albeit prioritized and based on better analysis), as opposed to confronting more forthrightly the possibility that the Bank may have reached the limits of potential effectiveness in these areas.

5. The Panel believes that there are a number of reasons why this may be so, which could have been further elaborated in the report. Civil service reform, for example, is limited by fiscal constraints that many countries face and by the growing mobility of skilled labor and competition from the private sector that have been brought about by economic development and globalization. Corruption is often driven by key political actors (who, on occasion, are members of governments that are clients of the Bank and whose behavior may not be corrected by anything that the Bank or other donors can offer). The report suggests that civil service reform and anticorruption and transparency efforts take a long time to germinate; it may be, however, that external donor interventions are permanently hostage to local and global conditions over which the donors have no control.

The IEG report provides an excellent analytical basis for understanding both the importance and functioning of PSR. Its evaluation of the Bank's recent work in this area is quite frank and suggests important new directions for future strategy. We fully support the Bank's focus on anticorruption, transparency, and good governance more generally.

Members of the External Advisory Panel

Shankar Acharya
Indian Council for Research on International Economic Relations

Francis Fukuyama
School for Advanced International Studies, Johns Hopkins University

Chapter 1

1. Updates of the strategy implementation were produced in 2003 and 2006 and shared with the Board.

2. The European Commission offers the following definition: "Governance refers to the rules, processes, and behavior by which interests are articulated, resources are managed, and power is exercised in society. The way public functions are carried out, public resources are managed, and public regulatory powers are exercised is the major issue to be addressed in that context" (European Commission 2006, p. 14).

3. The evaluation does not cover tax policy, because that is not directly related to how the government organizes itself.

4. In the SAP system coding of projects, this is the category called Anticorruption and Governance. Because governance also refers to a much wider agenda, however, including more than just the PSR topics treated here, and because the topics under the governance part of Anticorruption and Governance are mainly about transparency, this evaluation calls the category Anticorruption and Transparency.

5. This is similar to the one in the 2006 Public Sector Strategy Update, table 19.

Chapter 2

1. The word "governance" was added in 2003, making it the Public Sector and Governance Board.

2. "There is growing evidence that money lent for individual projects is, to some extent, fungible because it frees up government resources to be allocated elsewhere . . . " (World Bank 2000, p. xvii).

Chapter 3

1. The primary source of information in this chapter regarding World Bank PSR lending activities has been drawn from a list of projects carefully identified by the IEG team. The process used to select these projects is described in appendix A. These projects will sometimes be called "PSR projects." A complete list of the projects is provided in appendix B (http://www.worldbank.org/ieg/psr/appendix.html).

2. Of projects approved in 2000–06 that were managed by other sector boards, 89 percent were adjustment loans.

3. Of the 219 adjustment projects from 1998 to 2006 on the IEG list, the Public Sector (and Governance) Board managed 79 projects, the Economic Policy Board managed 88 projects, and other sector boards managed 52 projects.

4. PSR components made up 75–100 percent of 45 projects, 50–74 percent of 157 projects, and 1–49 percent of 201 projects.

5. On average, this is about $42.5 million per loan.

6. The number of PSR projects was the highest in fiscal 2005, with 59 projects, about 22 percent of all World Bank projects approved that year.

7. PSR lending per year was $429 million (nominal) in 1987–99 and $1,983 million per year in 2000–06. PSR lending was particularly high in fiscal 2002 (especially via IBRD loans) because of several large PSR loans to Turkey (two), Pakistan, Argentina, Russia, Mexico, and the Democratic Republic of the Congo.

8. The AAA section is based on the following evaluations: IEG 2007; World Bank 2003b, 2004c, 2005, 2006a; IMF 2006.

9. An Integrative Fiduciary Assessment integrates the work normally carried out through a PER, CPAR, and CFAA and may substitute for them. Comprehensive data on ESW and the PSR part of it are not available for years before 1999.

10. The Institutional Development Fund provides grants of up to $500,000 to help countries build capacity in specific agencies (typically just one per grant) to plan and implement policy reform and poverty-

reduction initiatives, promote sustainable economic development, and manage external assistance.

11. For IBRD countries, AAA seems to be largely demand driven.

12. There were no obvious differences in PSR packages between the blend and the full IDA countries.

13. Because IDA resources have a grant component and the countries have little or no access to market financing, the Bank presumably has more leverage with them than with the IBRD borrowers.

14. For the 21 IDA countries with initial governance CPIAs below 2.5, a larger share of cases (9) had no PSR lending. Nonetheless, the Bank stayed engaged at least to the extent of doing some AAA in all but three countries.

15. Only 4 of 62 had no PSR AAA or lending: Central African Republic, Sudan, Kirbati, and Vanuatu.

16. The number of projects with PFM components comprising 25 percent or more of the total amount increased from an average of 6 projects per year over the period 1990–99 (59 projects) to an average of 22 projects per year over the period 2000–06 (157 projects).

17. If one focuses only on projects with more than 25 percent in the PFM theme, the proportion of PFM adjustment loans increased from 31 to 67 percent over the respective periods (see appendix A).

18. The count of conditions here includes only those that were in projects with at least three conditions pertaining to the four PSR themes addressed in this report. One should be careful in using these numbers because the conditions vary in difficulty and importance, which is not reflected in the simple count of numbers given here.

19. About 56 percent of these were adjustment loans in 1990–99, and this increased to about 75 percent during the years 2000–06.

20. This is in contrast with the comparable data for the PFM theme—where there was a strong increase in the use of policy-based lending and only a modest increase in investment lending since 2002.

21. As discussed elsewhere in detail, much of the Bank's anticorruption "work" is not explicitly focused on anticorruption, but, instead is via other channels (including the other three themes). This discussion refers only to explicit anticorruption and governance components.

22. The percentage of PSR projects with PFM, CSA, and TAX components does not fall after 2000, even though the percentage of PSR projects with ACT projects increases significantly.

Chapter 4

1. The CPIA is an internal World Bank measure of each country's present policy and institutional framework, which is created annually by staff for essentially all countries with the potential to borrow. "'Quality' refers to how conducive that framework is to fostering poverty reduction, sustainable growth, and the effective use of development assistance. The CPIA ratings are used in the IDA allocation process and several other corporate activities" (from 2005 CPIA Questionnaire).

2. CPIA data before 1999 are not comparable to the current definitions. The World Bank Group has contributed a lot to the production and understanding of governance indicators (see World Bank 2007c and Levy 2007 for reviews of this work). Most of the indicators are about the political system, government stability, and the environment for the private sector—most of which are not the direct concerns of this evaluation.

3. The case studies did not include any countries where the Bank had no lending for PSR, so there is not solid evidence on these cases. There were examples in Chile, Guyana, India, Mexico, and Russia, where each country successfully pursued some important reforms without lending, but with AAA from the Bank or support from other donors.

4. The sample is based on the period in which the projects closed in order to reduce sample selection problems. If the evaluation had looked at the set of projects approved 1999–2006 and already closed and rated, then it would have excluded projects that were delayed in execution and extended. Because these would probably have been lower performing, the average rating would have been biased upward.

5. Projects are matched to the recipient country's CPIA score at project approval (for projects approved in 1999–2006; for others the 1999 CPIA is used).

6. Since the end of the evaluation period (fiscal 2006), the Mexico team completed an IGR with indepth analysis of political issues. The report used local academic consultants extensively and was an important

piece to inform the Country Partnership Strategy progress report and the forthcoming strategy.

Chapter 5

1. CPIA 14 for revenue administration includes tax policy and customs, as well as tax administration, which is the theme in the projects considered here.

2. Recognizes cash transactions only.

3. Recognizes transactions when commitments are made and accounts for depreciation of capital assets.

4. Audit measuring compliance with laws and regulations in the use of resources.

5. Audit measuring economy, efficiency, and effectiveness in the use of resources.

6. This approach is under active reconsideration by the Bank.

7. Public Expenditure and Institutional Review is now often the title.

8. The PEFA partnership includes the IMF, the European Commission, the UK's DFID, the French Ministry of Foreign Affairs, the Royal Norwegian Ministry of Foreign Affairs, the Swiss State Secretariat for Economic Affairs, and the Strategic Partnership for Africa. The PEFA secretariat is in the World Bank.

9. Outside the Bank, but used and supported by it, there is the Open Budget Initiative of the International Budget Project, which monitors and rates countries in detail for how well they give out public information on the formulation and execution of the budget (www. openbudgetindex.org). PEFA, by contrast, looks at the process internal to the government, so the two are complementary.

10. One of the countries, Pakistan, has conducted PEFAs at the provincial level for three of four provinces: http://www.pefa.org/about_test.htm.

11. PEFA is intended to motivate improvement in actual PFM, but this has not happened yet to an extent reflected in median CPIA ratings, which have not improved 2004–06 (or 1999–2006) for the majority of countries doing PEFA.

12. For instance, the Guinea-Bissau PER update (World Bank 2007b) looks extensively at the fiscal dimension of civil service reform, with no attention to performance, quality of personnel, recruitment, or public sector organization.

13. Both these indicators are designed to give cross-section rankings, so the change over time has ques-

tionable meaning, except in comparison to the countries with no PSR lending.

14. BEEPS is a Europe and Central Asia–specific variant of a number of enterprise surveys supported by the World Bank.

15. Benin, Bolivia, Brazil (Rio de Janeiro), Burundi, Colombia, Ecuador, Ghana, Guatemala, Guinea, Haiti, Honduras, Kenya, Madagascar, Malawi, Mozambique, Paraguay, Peru, Sierra Leone, and Zambia. http://web. worldbank.org/WBSITE/EXTERNAL/WBI/EXTWBIGO VANTCOR/0,,contentMDK:20726148~pagePK:64168445 ~piPK:64168309~theSitePK:1740530,00.html.

16. The Stolen Asset Recovery Project is a new initiative that the Bank has supported as an action against grand corruption. It has good potential for bringing stolen resources back to poor countries, and it has done so in some cases, such as Nigeria. It is too soon to judge the effects on corruption. Moreover, monitoring what happens with the repatriated assets has yet to be addressed.

17. Research by Khan and his coauthors has examined how different forms of corruption or rent seeking have different impacts on economic growth (for example, Khan and Komo 2000; Khan 2004).

Chapter 6

1. Hungary and Poland, which joined the European Union in 2004, did not improve their governance CPIAs from 1999 to 2006, because they were already high in 1999 because of earlier Bank-supported reforms. The Czech Republic and Estonia had already graduated from Bank lending and CPIA ratings by 2006, with high governance ratings.

2. Other evaluations, of lending to middle-income countries and of PRSCs, have and will examine the overall effectiveness of these instruments. This evaluation considers them only in relation to PSR support.

Appendix A

1. That is, "desired action" conditions were not included.

2. The team recognizes that the original coding of these percentages is imperfect in that they represent an approximation of the actual share of the program dedicated to PSR at project design and may differ from implementation.

Bates, Robert H. 2001. "Institutions and Economic Performance." In *The Institutional Foundations of a Market Economy*, ed. Gudrun Kochendorfer and Boris Pleskovic. Berlin and Washington, DC: Deutsche Stiftung fur International Entwicklung and World Bank.

Bird, Richard Miller, and Milka Casanegra de Jantscher. 1992. *Improving Tax Administration in Developing Countries.* Washington, DC: International Monetary Fund.

Brumby, Jim. 1999. "Budgeting Reforms in OECD Member Countries." In *Managing Government Expenditure*, eds. Salvatore Schiavo-Campo and Daniel Tommasi, 349–62. Manila: Asian Development Bank.

Collier, Paul. 2007. *The Bottom Billion: Why the Poorest Countries Are Failing and What Can Be Done About It.* Oxford: Oxford University Press.

Craig, David, and Doug Porter. 2003. "Poverty Reduction Strategy Papers: A New Convergence." *World Development* 31(1): 53–69.

de Renzio, Paolo, and William Dorotinsky. 2007. "Tracking Progress in the Quality of PFM Systems in HIPCs—An Update on Past Assessments Using PEFA Data." Washington, DC: PEFA Secretariat.

DFID (Department for International Development). n.d. "Public Expenditure Tracking Surveys." http://www.dfid.gov.uk/aboutdfid/organisation/pfma/pfma-pets.pdf.

Dove, Suzanne. 2002. "Fragile Miracles: The Creation and Sustainability of Autonomous Oversight Agencies in a Politicized Bureaucracy." Working paper, Universitat Autonoma de Barcelona.

Economist. 2007. "Corruption: Rules of the Road." 5 May: 92.

European Commission. 2006. *Thematic Evaluation of the EC Support to Good Governance: Final Report.* Brussels: European Commission.

Gill, Jit B. S. 2000. "A Diagnostic Framework for Revenue Administration." Technical Paper No. 472, World Bank, Washington, DC.

Golden, Mirian, and Lucio Picci. 2005. "Proposal for a New Measure of Corruption Illustrated Using Italian Data." *Economics and Politics* 17 (1): 37–75.

IDD & Associates. 2006. *Evaluation of General Budget Support: Synthesis Report.* Birmingham, U.K.: University of Birmingham.

IEG (Independent Evaluation Group). 2007. "Country Financial Accountability Assessments and Country Procurement Assessment Reports: How Effective Are World Bank Fiduciary Diagnostics?" Report No. CODE2007-0010, World Bank, Washington, DC.

———. 2006a. *Debt Relief for the Poorest: An Evaluation Update of the HIPC Initiative.* IEG Study Series. Washington, DC: World Bank.

———. 2006b. *Engaging with Fragile States: An IEG Review of World Bank Support to Low-Income Countries Under Stress.* IEG Study Series. Washington, DC: World Bank.

———. 2005. *Capacity Building in Africa: An Evaluation of World Bank Support.* IEG Study Series. Washington, DC: World Bank.

———. 2004a. "An Evaluation of World Bank Assistance to Transition Economies." Report No. 29761, World Bank, Washington, DC.

———. 2004b. "Mainstreaming Anti-Corruption Activities in World Bank Assistance: A Review of Progress since 1997." Report No. 29620, World Bank, Washington, DC.

———. 1999. "Civil Service Reform: A Review of World Bank Assistance." Report No. 19599, World Bank, Washington, DC.

———. 1998. "The Impact of Public Expenditure Reviews: An Evaluation." Report No. 18573, World Bank, Washington, DC.

IMF (International Monetary Fund). 2006. "Selected African Countries: IMF Technical Assistance

Evaluation—Public Expenditure Management and Reform." IMF Country Report No. 06/67, Washington, DC.

IMF and World Bank. 2002. "Actions to Strengthen the Tracking of Poverty-Reducing Public Spending in Heavily Indebted Poor Countries." PREM Paper, IMF and World Bank, Washington, DC.

Islam, Roumeen. 2003. "Do More Transparent Governments Govern Better?" Policy Research Working Paper No. 3077, World Bank, Washington, DC.

Kaufmann, Daniel, Aart Kraay, and Massimo Mastruzzi. 2005. "Governance Matters IV: Governance Indicators for 1996–2004." Policy Research Working Paper No. 3630, World Bank, Washington, DC.

Khan, Mushtaq H. 2004. "State Failure in Developing Countries and Strategies of Institutional Reform." In *Annual World Bank Conference on Development Economics Europe: Toward Pro-Poor Policies: Aid Institutions and Globalization,* ed. B. Tungodden, N. Stern, and I. Kolstad, 165–95. Oxford, U.K., and Washington, DC: Oxford University Press and World Bank.

Khan, Mushtaq H., and K. S. Komo, eds. 2000. *Rents, Rent-Seeking, and Economic Development: Theory and Evidence in Asia.* Cambridge, U.K.: Cambridge University Press.

Lele, Uma. 1975. *The Design of Rural Development: Lessons from Africa.* Baltimore, MD: Johns Hopkins University Press.

Levy, Brian. 2007. *Governance Reform: Bridging Monitoring and Action.* Washington, DC: World Bank.

Levy, Brian, and Sahr Kpundeh, eds. 2004. *Building State Capacity in Africa: New Approaches, Emerging Lessons.* Washington, DC: World Bank Institute.

Mallaby, Sebastian. 2004. *The World's Banker.* New York: Penguin Press.

Mason, Edward, and Robert Asher. 1973. *The World Bank and Bretton Woods.* Washington, DC: The Brookings Institution.

North, Douglass. 1990. *Institutions, Institutional Change and Economic Performance.* New York: Cambridge University Press.

OECD (Organisation for Economic Co-operation and Development). 1995. *Budgeting for Results: Perspectives on Public Expenditure Management.* Paris: OECD.

Oxford Policy Management. 2000. *Medium-Term Expenditure Frameworks—Panacea or Danger-ous Distraction?* Oxford, U.K.: Oxford Policy Management.

Parison, Neil. 2005. "World Bank Public Sector Strategy Implementation: Case Studies of Bangladesh, Brazil, Cambodia, Guatemala, India Karnataka, and Indonesia." Main Report Draft, World Bank, Washington, DC.

Paul, Samuel. 1990. "Institutional Reforms in Sector Adjustment Operations: The World Bank's Experience." World Bank Discussion Paper 92, World Bank, Washington, DC.

PEFA (Public Expenditure and Financial Accountability) Secretariat. 2005. "Public Financial Management Performance Measurement Framework." http://www.pefa.org/about_test.htm.

Pollitt, Christopher, and Geert Bouchaert. 2004. *Public Management Reform: A Comparative Analysis,* rev. ed. Oxford, U.K.: Oxford University Press.

Przeworski, Adam, Michael E. Alvarez, Jose Antonio Cheibub, and Fernando Limongi. 2000. *Democracy and Development: Political Institutions and Well-Being in the World, 1950–1990.* Cambridge, U.K.: Cambridge University Press.

Reinikka, R., and J. Svensson. 2006. "Using Micro-Surveys to Measure and Explain Corruption." *World Development* 34 (2): 359–70.

Rubin, Irene S., and Joanne Kelly. 2005. "Budget and Accounting Reforms." In *The Oxford Handbook of Public Management,* ed. Ewan Ferlie, Laurence E. Lynn, Jr., and Christopher Pollitt, 562–90. Oxford, U.K.: Oxford University Press.

Schick, Allen. 1998. "Why Most Developing Countries Should Not Try New Zealand´s Reforms." *The World Bank Research Observer* 13 (1): 123–31.

Shand, David. 2001. "Changing Perspectives in the World Bank on Asia and Other Regions." In *Learning from International Public Management Reform,* ed. Lawrence Jones, James Guthrie, and Peter Steane, 377–90. Oxford, U.K.: JAI-Elsevier Science.

Stevens, Mike, and Stefanie Teggemann. 2004. "Comparative Experience with Public Service Reform in Ghana, Tanzania and Zambia." In *Building State Capacity in Africa: New Approaches, Emerging Lessons,* ed. Brian Levy and Sahr Kpundeh, Washington, DC: World Bank.

Thomas, M.A. 2007. "The Governance Bank." *International Affairs* 83 (4): 729–45.

United Republic of Tanzania. 1996. "Report on the Commission on Corruption (the Warioba Report)." Dar es Salaam: Government of Tanzania.

van de Walle, Nicolas. 2001. *African Economies and the Politics of Permanent Crisis.* New York: Cambridge University Press.

Wescott, C. 2006. "Adapting Asia Pacific Public Administration to a Globalizing World: Some Lessons from Experience." In *Handbook of Globalization, Governance, and Public Administration,* ed. Ali Farazmand and Jack Pinkowski. New York: Dekker Publishing.

Wolfensohn, James. 1996. "Cancer of Corruption." Presentation at World Bank Annual Meeting, Washington, DC, October 1.

World Bank. 2007a. "Conditionality in Development Policy Lending." World Bank Paper No. SecM2007-0490, World Bank, Washington, DC.

———. 2007b. "Guinea-Bissau PER Update: Enhancing Growth and Fiscal Adjustment through Civil Service Reform." World Bank, Washington, DC.

———. 2007c. "Strengthening the World Bank Engagement on Governance and Anticorruption." Report No. 39055, World Bank, Washington, DC.

———. 2006a. "Economic and Sector Work Progress Report, IDA." Washington, DC.

———. 2006b. Ghana External Review of PFM. Vol. 2 Public Finance Management Performance Report and Performance Indicators.

———. 2006c. *Global Monitoring Report 2006: Strengthening Mutual Accountability, Aid, Trade, and Governance.* Washington, DC: World Bank.

———. 2006d. "The IDF FY02–05. An Independent Evaluation." OPCS Report, Washington, DC.

———. 2006e. "Mapping HIPC Expenditure Tracking Indicators to PEFA Public Financial Management Performance Indicators." www1.worldbank.org/publicsector/pe/StrengthenedApproach/MappingHIPC.pdf.

———. 2006f. "United Republic of Tanzania: Public Expenditure and Financial Accountability Review—FY05." Report No. 36642-TZ, World Bank, Washington, DC.

———. 2006g. "Review of Development Policy Lending: Review of PMF Issues and Fiduciary Arrangements." Financial Management Sector Board Report, World Bank, Washington, DC.

———. 2004a. "The Costs of Corruption." http://web.worldbank.org/WBSITE/EXTERNAL/NEWS/0,,contentMDK:20190187~menuPK:34457~pagePK:34370~piPK:34424~theSitePK:4607,00.html.

———. 2004b. "From Adjustment Lending to Development Policy Lending: Update of World Bank Policy." Working Paper No. R2004-0135, World Bank, Washington, DC.

———. 2004c. "Improving the Bank's Analytical and Advisory Services Progress Report." Washington, DC.

———. 2004d. "Public Expenditure Accountability in Africa: Progress, Lessons, and Challenges." In *Building State Capacity in Africa: New Approaches, Emerging Lessons,* ed. Brian Levy and Sahr Kpundeh, 179–209. Washington DC: World Bank.

———. 2004e. *World Development Report: Making Services Work for Poor People.* Washington, DC: World Bank.

———. 2003. "Bangladesh: Country Assistance Strategy Progress Report." Report No. 25886-BD, World Bank, Washington, DC.

———. 2002. "Reforming Public Institutions and Strengthening Governance: A World Bank Strategy, Implementation Update." Public Sector Governance Board Report, World Bank, Washington, DC.

———. 2001. "Guidelines for the World Bank's Work on Public Expenditure Analysis and Support (including PERs)." Draft Report, World Bank, Washington, DC.

———. 2000. *Reforming Public Institutions and Strengthening Governance: A World Bank Strategy.* Washington, DC: World Bank.

———. 1999. "Cambodia Public Expenditure Review: Enhancing the Effectiveness of Public Expenditures." Report No. 18791-KH, World Bank, Washington, DC.

———. 1998a. *Assessing Aid: What Works, What Doesn't, and Why.* New York: Oxford University Press.

———. 1998b. *Public Expenditure Management Handbook.* Washington, DC: World Bank.

———. 1997a. *Helping Countries Combat Corruption: The Role of the World Bank.* Washington, DC: World Bank.

———. 1997b. *World Development Report: The State in a Changing World.* New York and Washington, DC: Oxford University Press and World Bank.

———. 1995. *Bureaucrats in Business: The Economics and Politics of Government Ownership.* Washington, DC, and New York: World Bank and Oxford University Press.

———. 1994a. "Cambodia—From Rehabilitation to Reconstruction: An Economic Report." Report No. 12667, World Bank, Washington, DC.

———. 1994b. "Civil Service Reform in Latin America and the Caribbean: Proceedings of a Conference." Technical Paper No. 259, World Bank, Washington, DC.

———. 1992a. *Governance and Development.* Washington, DC: World Bank.

———. 1992b. "Effective Implementation: Key to Development Impact." Portfolio Management Task Force Report, World Bank, Washington, DC.

———. 1990. *Report on Adjustment Lending II: Policies for the Recovery of Growth.* Washington, DC: World Bank.

———. 1989. *From Crisis to Sustainable Growth: A Long-Term Perspective Study of Sub-Saharan Africa.* Washington, DC: World Bank.

———. 1983. *World Development Report: Management in Development.* New York and Washington, DC: Oxford University Press and World Bank.

———. 1981. *Accelerated Development in Sub-Saharan Africa: An Agenda for Action.* Washington, DC: World Bank.

World Bank and ADB (Asian Development Bank). 2003. *Cambodia: Enhancing Service Delivery through Improved Resource Allocation and Institutional Reform—Integrated Fiduciary Assessment and Public Expenditure Review.* Phnom Penh and Washington, DC: ADB and World Bank.

World Bank and IMF. 2006. "Heavily Indebted Poor Countries (HIPC) Initiative and Multilateral Debt Relief Initiative (MDRI)—Status of Implementation." World Bank and IMF, Washington, DC.

———. 2004. *Public Expenditure Management Country Assessment and Action Plan (AAP)—Ghana.* Washington, DC: World Bank and IMF.

———. 2003. *Bank/Fund Collaboration on Public Expenditure Issues.* Washington, DC: World Bank and IMF.

———. 2002. *Civil Service Reform: Strengthening World Bank and IMF Collaboration.* Washington, DC: World Bank and IMF. http://go.worldbank.org/Q2O3DQ5EF0.